Reading Advantage 4

Second Edition

Casey Malarcher

THOMSON

HEINLE

Australia · Canada · Mexico · Singapore · Spain · United Kingdom · United States

THOMSON
HEINLE

Reading Advantage, Second Edition, Student Book 4

Casey Malarcher

Publisher, Global ELT: Christopher Wenger
Editorial Manager: Sean Bermingham
Development Editor: Derek Mackrell
Production Editor: Tan Jin Hock
ELT Directors: John Lowe (Asia), Jim Goldstone (Latin America—ELT), Francisco Lozano (Latin America—Academic and Training, ELT)

Director of Marketing, ESL/ELT: Amy Mabley
Senior Marketing Manager: Ian Martin
Interior/Cover Design: Christopher Hanzie, TYA Inc.
Composition: Stella Tan, TYA Inc.
Cover Images: PhotoDisc, Inc.
Printer: Seng Lee Press

Printed in Singapore
1 2 3 4 5 6 7 8 9 10   08 07 06 05 04

For more information, contact Thomson Heinle, 25 Thomson Place, Boston, Massachusetts 02210 USA, or you can visit our Internet site at http://www.heinle.com

ISBN 1-4130-0117-3

Credits

Unless otherwise stated, all photos are from PhotoDisc, Inc. Digital Imagery © copyright 2004 PhotoDisc, Inc. The artwork on page 5 is the exclusive property of Heinle. Photos from other sources: page 13: Associated Press/Christie's; page 17: North Wind Picture Archives; page 27 and 39: EPA/Landov; page 35 and 71: Index Stock; page 43: Digital Vision; page 65, 75, and 87: Reuters/Landov; page 79: Bettmann/CORBIS; page 83: Kyodo/Landov

Dictionary definitions are adapted from Heinle's *Newbury House Dictionary of American English*, © 2002, Monroe Allen Publishers, Inc.
Sources of information: http://members.aol.com/AspireA1/ (Unit 1); http://news.bbc.co.uk/2/hi/health/2732505.stm & http://www.who.int/medicines/library/trm/trm_strat_eng.pdf (Unit 2); http://www.artchive.com/artchive/K/kahlo.html (Unit 3); http://en.wikipedia.org/wiki/Indo-European & http://www.wordorigins.org/histeng.htm (Unit 4); http://www.takaratoys.co.jp/english/PR/Meowlingual.pdf (Unit 5); http://www.yourdictionary.com/library/article004.html (Review 1–5); http://sunsite.au.ac.th/thailand/special_event/moon/ & http://www.gftours.com.tw/html/gft-03.htm (Unit 6); http://www.bts.gov/publications/national_transportation_ statistics/2002/index.html, *The Times (London),* September 29, 2003, "Number of cars set to triple as global love affair continues apace," & http://en.wikipedia.org/wiki/Automobile's_impact_on_America (Unit 7); http://www.pbs.org/treasuresoftheworld/a_nav/boro_nav/main_borofrm.html (Unit 8); http://www.ananova.com/entertainment/story/sm_777072.html (Unit 9); http://www.ajc.state.ak.us/reports/cjcAppendixC.pdf & http://en.wikipedia.org/wiki/Punishment (Unit 13); http://www.showgate.com/tango.history.html, http://www.tango.spb.ru/eng/history.phtml, & http://www.todotango.com/english/biblioteca/cronicas/tango_en_japon.asp (Unit 14); http://www.amonline.net.au/thylacine/15.htm (Unit 15); http://en.wikipedia.org/wiki/Mammoth (Review 11–15); http://www.cpamedia.com/history/jim_thompson_thailand_silk_king/ (Unit 16); http://news.bbc.co.uk/1/hi/entertainment/tv_and_radio/3081604.stm (Unit 17); http://abcnews.go.com/sections/us/WolfFiles/wolffiles200.html, http://www.altonweb.com/history/wadlow/, & http://www.chinatown-online.com/china/facts/worldmost/worldmost.shtml (Unit 18); http://clio.fivecolleges.edu/smith/berenson/ (Unit 19); http://www.forbes.com/2003/10/23/cx_ld_deadcelebtear.html (Unit 20); http://en.wikipedia.org/wiki/Houdini (Review 16–20)

Contents

Preface

Welcome to *Reading Advantage Book 4*! In this book, you will find readings and exercises to help build your English vocabulary and reading skills. Each of the units in this book is divided into seven parts. These parts should be studied together to help you develop reading skills, as well as review new vocabulary and reinforce vocabulary presented in other units.

Before You Read
This part of each unit presents questions for you to think about before you read the passage. The questions focus on knowledge you may already have on the subject of the passage, as well as questions which will be answered in the reading. You should discuss (or write) the answers to these questions before reading.

Target Vocabulary
In this section, you are introduced to words from the reading that you may not know. You should be able to match the words with the simple definitions provided. After studying these words, continue with the reading.

Reading Passage
Each reading passage in Book 4 is around 650 words in length. First read this passage alone silently. At the end of each passage, the word count for the readings is shown, with a space to record your reading time for the passage. By keeping track of your reading times, using the chart inside the back cover of this book, you will be able to see the improvement in your reading speeds over the course. Each reading is recorded on the audio cassette/CD; after reading through silently, listen to the passage spoken by a native English speaker.

Reading Comprehension
This section is a series of multiple-choice questions about the passage. You are encouraged to look back at the reading in order to check your answers to these questions. The questions cover important reading skills, such as understanding the main idea, scanning for details, and reading for inference.

Idioms
This section highlights three idioms from the reading passage. The meaning of these idioms and examples of how they may be used are presented.

Vocabulary Reinforcement
This section is divided into two parts. Section A has eight multiple-choice sentences for vocabulary and idiom practice. Section B presents a cloze passage with missing words to complete using the correct form of vocabulary items from the box. Vocabulary and idioms tested in this section have been selected from the present unit, as well as earlier units in the book.

What Do You Think?
In this section, you are encouraged to think further about what you have read and communicate your own ideas and feelings about the topics presented. Answers to these questions can be used as a writing activity.

There are also four review units in this book—one after every five units. These will help you to check what you have learned.

I hope you enjoy using *Reading Advantage*!

Casey Malarcher

The Story of Numbers 1

Before You Read

Answer the following questions.

1. Are there any numbers that you think are lucky or unlucky? What are they, and why?

_____

2. Do you think that someone's name says something about their personality?

_____

3. Would you say that you are a superstitious person?

_____

Target Vocabulary

Match each word with the best meaning.

1. _____ ambitious
2. _____ assign
3. _____ daring
4. _____ diplomatic
5. _____ doubt
6. _____ enthusiastic
7. _____ insight
8. _____ obtain
9. _____ practical
10. _____ superstition

a. get (by buying or being given)
b. sensible; not foolish
c. showing skill at handling people sensitively
d. to be unsure, but not believe (v); uncertainty (n)
e. eager; excited
f. wanting success
g. brave; courageous
h. belief in things that are not real or possible, such as magic
i. ability to see or know the truth
j. give a job or task to someone or something; decide that something has a particular meaning or value

Do you believe that some numbers are lucky or unlucky? If you answered yes to this question, you are certainly not alone. **Superstitions** about numbers are common in many societies. For example, many people in Western countries believe that the number 13 is unlucky. They believe 13 people should never sit at a table together, and that terrible things will happen on Friday the 13th. Some buildings do not even **assign** a 13th floor. Similarly, in Chinese and Japanese culture, the number 4, which sounds like the word for "death," is often considered unlucky. On the other hand, 7 is considered a lucky number in Western countries. In China, 8 is a lucky number because it sounds like the word "prosper."[1]

In ancient times, it was quite common to believe in the magical power of numbers. It was believed some numbers could let you know the future or show the hidden side of a person's personality. Numerology, the art of reading the power in numbers, was often practiced in Jewish tradition and among Greek mathematicians. Today, many of those who still practice numerology use a system that equates each letter of the alphabet to one of the numbers 1 through 8.

Here is an example of how this system of numerology works. In order to find the number related to a person's name, first assign the correct number to each letter of the name, using the following chart.

| 1 A • I • Q • J • Y | 3 C • G • L • S | 5 E • H • N | 7 O • Z |
| 2 B • K • R | 4 D • T • M | 6 U • V • W • X | 8 F • P |

For example, take the name John: J = 1, O = 7, H = 5, and N = 5. Add these numbers together to give a total of 18. Because 18 is larger than 9, add the two digits, so that 1 + 8 = 9. Therefore, 9 is the number that represents the name John.

Each number from 1 to 9 shows a different type of personality. One is the number of a leader, someone who is **ambitious**, independent, and self-sufficient,[2] but who might have a tendency to be bossy. Two represents a person who is supportive, **diplomatic**, and analytical. This person makes a good partner, but may tend to be lonely. Three is a social person who is outgoing, **enthusiastic**, sociable, and enjoys life. On the negative side, this number person may lack self-discipline. A person whose name equals four is **practical**, traditional, and serious. They work hard to get things done, but may be uncomfortable when they don't have a routine. Fives are adventurous, **daring**, and good at getting people to go along with them. However, they tend to get bored easily. Six is a "happy" number. This type of person is peaceful, caring, and reliable. On the negative side, they may sometimes end up feeling taken advantage of. Seven is the number for a person who prefers to be alone. This kind of person is a thinker, and is often quite spiritual. On the other hand, they may be worried about not being good enough. Eight shows a person who is good with money, and can be quite decisive. On the other hand, this kind of person can tend to lack empathy for other people. Nine is the number of someone who is creative and multi-talented,[3] and wants to improve the world. This person would make a good community leader, but needs to take care of small details as well as looking at the big picture.

Is there any truth to numerology? Although very popular, it has never been scientifically proven, and skeptics[4] **doubt** it has any validity at all. They ask, "If numerology is universally true, then how does it account for variations in the number **obtained** for an object or person, from translating a word between different languages?" Still, for many people, numerology remains a very entertaining way to get some **insight** into your personality.

_____ **minutes** _____ **seconds** (681 words)

---

[1] **prosper** to grow in wealth
[2] **self-sufficient** independent; able to meet one's needs by oneself. The prefix "self-" means "related to oneself."
[3] **multi-talented** having many talents. The prefix "multi-" means "many."
[4] **skeptic** a person who doubts or doesn't believe

Reading Comprehension

Circle the letter of the best answer.

1. What is the main idea of this passage?

   a. why people believe in numerology

   b. how people use numerology to tell someone's personality

   c. reasons why numerology is not scientific

   d. why certain numbers are unlucky

2. Which of these is NOT an example of a superstition?

   a. The number 13 is unlucky.

   b. The number 4 sounds like the word for "death."

   c. The number 8 is unlucky.

   d. A person's name can reveal their personality.

3. According to this passage, what would be the number for Mary Lee?

   a. 2   **b.** 3   **c.** 4   **d.** 8

4. According to the passage, what number person would make the best explorer?

   a. 2   **b.** 4   **c.** 5   **d.** 6

5. Which of these statements would a skeptic be most likely to agree with?

   a. Numerology shows that John would make a good community leader.

   b. Numerology is nothing but superstition.

   c. Numerology is a good way to gain insight into someone's personality.

   d. Different languages require different kinds of numerology.

Idioms

Find each idiom in the story.

1. **go along with**—*support; agree with*
   * Marsh did not **go along with** the president's new program.
   * It's a good idea. I can **go along with** that.

2. **the big picture**—*the whole situation*
   * He only looks at small details; he never sees **the big picture**.
   * To be a good manager, you need to look at **the big picture**.

3. **tend to/have a tendency to**—*be likely to; prefer to; often do*
   * Hotel prices **tend to** go up during the holiday season.
   * He **has a tendency to** give up if something is too difficult.

Vocabulary Reinforcement

A. Circle the letter of the word or phrase that best completes the sentence.

1. In theory, working only four days a week is a great idea, but in reality, it just isn't _____.
   a. diplomatic   **b.** practical   **c.** ambitious   **d.** daring

2. Fay is so much fun to be around. She's always so _____.
   a. practical   **b.** disciplined   **c.** enthusiastic   **d.** ambitious

3. Even if you don't agree with people, you need to be _____ or you might sound rude.
   a. diplomatic   **b.** daring   **c.** gone along with   **d.** ambitious

4. On the surface, his decision seems like a mistake, but looking at _____ it was the right choice.
   a. multi-talented   **b.** superstition   **c.** routine   **d.** the big picture

5. Sam never makes up his own mind. He always just _____ what other people decide.
   a. tends to   **b.** sets apart   **c.** goes along with   **d.** tracks down

6. The firefighter ran into the burning building to save the child in a _____ rescue.
   a. controversial   **b.** daring   **c.** practical   **d.** messy

7. If you want to succeed in life you need to be _____, and get ahead of other people.
   a. ambitious   **b.** conservative   **c.** creative   **d.** traditional

8. I know many people believe in ghosts, but personally, I _____ they are real.
   a. prove   **b.** am superstitious   **c.** skeptic   **d.** doubt

B. Complete the passage with the correct form of items from the box. One item is extra.

assign	tend to	go along with	insight	superstition	doubt	obtain

Many people think that numerology is only (1)_____ and (2)_____
that there is any truth to it. Some people, however, believe that numbers can give
(3)_____ into a person's character or life. They say that people's names can be
related to numbers, and people with the same number (4)_____ have similar
personalities. In order to (5)_____ the number related to a person's name, you
first (6)_____ a number from one to eight to each letter in the name. By adding
these numbers in a certain way, you can discover what number a person is, and find out
about their personality.

What Do You Think?

1. According to the numerology chart, what number represents you? Do you think the description of this number matches your personality?

2. Do you know of any other superstitions? Do you think that there is any truth to them?

Traditional Medicine 2

Before You Read

Answer the following questions.

1. Do you know of any plants that are useful as medicine?

   _____

   _____

   _____

2. In your country, besides doctors and the hospital, where can people go for help if they are sick?

   _____

   _____

   _____

3. What can people in your country do if they are sick and cannot afford a doctor?

   _____

   _____

   _____

Target Vocabulary

Match each word with the best meaning.

1. _____ adopt
2. _____ endangered
3. _____ global
4. _____ harvest
5. _____ policy
6. _____ remedy
7. _____ resistant
8. _____ strategy
9. _____ sustain
10. _____ therapy

a. general plan; set of rules

b. to copy or begin a new idea or plan; also, make someone else's child legally yours

c. planning in order to achieve a goal

d. relating to all the world; worldwide

e. treatment of medical and mental illnesses, usually without surgery

f. to keep in existence

g. not able to be touched or hurt by something

h. medicine that cures an illness (n); to fix or repair (v)

i. in danger of being wiped out or killed

j. gather a crop (plants grown for use by people) (v); such a crop that has been gathered (n)

In 1974, the United Nations World Health Organization (WHO) **adopted** a new **policy**. WHO tried to encourage developing countries[1] to develop their own traditional forms of medicine, instead of turning to Western medicine for expensive cures to medical problems. There were many people who looked down on this new policy, but WHO felt it was the most reasonable solution to the large health
5   problems facing poor countries. Today, WHO estimates that a third of the global population lack easy access to modern drugs, and that in the poorest parts of Africa and Asia, that figure rises to fifty percent. WHO believed that the people in developing countries who could not afford or find modern medical doctors were better off using traditional medicine rather than no medicine at all.

Today, traditional medicine and treatments are not only used in developing countries, but are
10   increasing in popularity in North America and Europe. In the United Kingdom, for example, US$230 million is spent on traditional **remedies** annually. In China, traditional herbal medicines account for thirty to fifty percent of all medicines used. The **global** market for traditional medicines is estimated to be $60 billion, and growing every year.

Twenty-five percent of modern medicines are made from plants that were first used in traditional
15   medicine, and scientists believe they have just scratched the surface. For example, one Chinese herbal remedy, which has been used for two thousand years, has recently been found to be effective against varieties of malaria that have **resistance** to other drugs. This herb could end up saving a million lives a year, mostly among children. In South Africa, another traditional plant is being used to treat patients with AIDS.

20   Recognizing the importance of traditional medicines, in 2003 WHO launched a Traditional Medicine **Strategy**. Among the recommendations of this strategy, there were several areas of concern. The first area of concern is safety. WHO recommends more scientific testing on traditional medicine—not all traditional medicines are as helpful as the two mentioned above, and some can actually be harmful. For example, in the United States, a traditional Chinese herb, Ma Huang, was sold as a diet drug. It
25   was to blame for many heart attacks and at least a dozen deaths. In Belgium, at least seventy people received liver damage when they took a herbal remedy made from the wrong species of plant.

Another area of concern is biodiversity[2] and **sustainability**. Some people are worried that as herbal medicines become more popular, the plants that these medicines are made from may become endangered as they are over-**harvested**. For example, in eastern and southern Africa a species of wild
30   potato has become **endangered** because of reports that it is effective in the treatment of AIDS.

There is also the problem of rights to drugs created from traditional remedies. Research into traditional remedies is increasingly being done by large drug companies, mostly based in Western countries. There is a fear that as these companies produce drugs they will claim to have the rights to the medicine. WHO recognizes that there is a need to make sure that any profits from drugs produced
35   from traditional medicines are shared with the local culture from which the medicine originated.

Traditional treatments don't only include medicines, they also include such treatments as acupuncture (using needles to treat illnesses) and aromatherapy (which, as the name suggests, uses types of smell as **therapy**). Acupuncture, for example, started in China, but is now performed in more than seventy countries around the world. There are at least 50,000 acupuncturists in Asia alone, and another
40   15,000 in Europe, and 12,000 in the United States. Even conventional doctors have come to recognize the benefits of acupuncture to stop pain and to treat some illnesses. In the United Kingdom, almost half of all conventional doctors either recommend acupuncture in some cases, or will perform acupuncture themselves. In fact, several British soccer players have used acupuncture to treat injuries that, in the past, would have required surgery, or that they would have just had to put up with.

 _____ **minutes** _____ **seconds** (673 words)

---

[1] **developing countries** countries that are poor and have few industries
[2] **biodiversity** the prefix "bio" means "life." Biodiversity means a diversity of living things.

Reading Comprehension

Circle the letter of the best answer.

1. What is this passage mainly about?
   a. why traditional medicine is so effective
   b. a program to increase the use of alternative medicine around the world
   c. the main differences between traditional and conventional medicines
   d. the history and future of the World Health Organization

2. Why does WHO encourage developing countries to use traditional medicines?
   a. Non-traditional medicines are often too expensive.
   b. Traditional medicine is usually more effective.
   c. Western countries shouldn't have to supply drugs to developing countries.
   d. The populations of developing countries prefer traditional medicines.

3. According to the passage, which of these can be treated by acupuncture?
   a. being overweight   c. malaria
   b. AIDS   d. pain

4. Which of these statements would WHO probably agree with?
   a. Herbal remedies are much safer than conventional medicine.
   b. In the future, more Western drugs will be based on traditional plants.
   c. Western companies should own any species they produce drugs from.
   d. Conventional doctors should avoid using traditional medicine.

5. Which of these does the passage NOT mention as one of WHO's main concerns?
   a. species protection   c. sharing of profits with local cultures
   b. drug safety   d. problems caused by acupuncture

Idioms

Find each idiom in the story.

1. **be better (worse) off**—*benefit; be more (less) successful*
   • John **was better off** living with his parents than living alone.
   • You'll **be better off** trying to solve this problem together.

2. **put up with**—*accept or tolerate something, even though it is unpleasant*
   • I hate having to **put up with** a lot of noise when I'm trying to work.
   • I don't know how she **puts up with** her boyfriend. She should leave him.

3. **scratch the surface**— *deal with a problem or subject in a very shallow way,*
   without understanding it completely
   • This is a very complicated problem, and scientists have just **scratched the surface**.
   • I thought I understood the subject, but I've really only **scratched the surface**.

Vocabulary Reinforcement

A. Circle the letter of the word or phrase that best completes the sentence.

1. Unless something is done to help them, many _____ species in South America will die out completely.
   a. resistant   **b.** enthusiastic   **c.** global   **d.** endangered

2. Many farms need to hire extra workers when it is time to _____.
   a. harvest   **b.** sustain   **c.** grow   **d.** perform

3. I don't like our new boss either, but we'll just have to _____ him.
   a. turn to   **b.** be worse off with   **c.** put up with   **d.** wipe out

4. It's difficult for a teacher to _____ her students' interest for a whole semester.
   a. sustain   **b.** resist   **c.** account for   **d.** recognize

5. Police have arrested over a hundred tax cheats this year, and they've just _____.
   a. been worse off   **b.** gone along with it   **c.** had a tendency   **d.** scratched the surface

6. The birds on the island had never seen cats before, and had no _____ to their attacks.
   a. sustainability   **b.** remedies   **c.** therapy   **d.** resistance

7. The team had a meeting to decide their _____ for the match on Saturday.
   a. strategy   **b.** therapy   **c.** policy   **d.** rights

8. After Meg's parents were killed, she was _____ by her uncle and aunt.
   a. sustained   **b.** endangered   **c.** adopted   **d.** harvested

B. Complete the passage with the correct form of items from the box. One item is extra.

global	put up with	policy	therapy	remedies	adopted	better off

The World Health Organization recognizes the importance of traditional medicines, and the organization's (1)_____ recommends that developing countries use more of these medicines. WHO has (2)_____ this policy because conventional medicines are often too expensive for developing countries to buy. WHO says these countries are (3)_____ treating people with traditional medicines rather than doing nothing at all. Also, people in Western countries are now recognizing the benefits of these (4)_____. For example, it is becoming increasingly common for European and American doctors to use acupuncture (5)_____ with their patients. Overall, the (6)_____ market for traditional medicine is worth billions of dollars annually, and growing every year.

What Do You Think?

1. What are the pros and cons of alternative medicine compared to conventional medicine?

2. Do you know of any other types of alternative medicine? Which are used in your country? Which have you tried?

Frida Kahlo

Before You Read

Answer the following questions.

1. Are there any famous female artists in your country? What do you know about them?

   _____

   _____

   _____

2. Look at the painting on the left. How would you describe the person in the picture?

   _____

   _____

   _____

3. Do you know of any people who have overcome physical problems to become successful?

   _____

   _____

   _____

Target Vocabulary

Match each word with the best meaning.

1. _____ activist
2. _____ appreciate
3. _____ commit suicide
4. _____ congratulate
5. _____ critic
6. _____ influence
7. _____ inspire
8. _____ severe
9. _____ typical
10. _____ undergo

a. a person who reviews and gives opinions about art, movies, books, music, etc.

b. very serious; very strong

c. kill oneself

d. to cause someone to work hard or be creative

e. usual; representative

f. be thankful for; understand the value and importance of (something)

g. have an effect on (v); an effect (n)

h. praise someone for doing something well, or for being successful

i. experience something necessary or unpleasant

j. person who works to change something, especially politics

When Mexican artist Frida Kahlo's paintings were put on display in a gallery in London, one art **critic** suggested that the exhibition walls should be covered with asbestos![1] Another poet and essayist described her paintings as "a ribbon around a bomb"—a quote that went on to provide the title for a documentary about her life. Such extraordinary comments about her work seem to
5 suggest Kahlo had a big impact on the art world of her time. Sadly, this is not the case. Kahlo's work was not widely **appreciated** during her life, and she is actually a much bigger name today than she was during her lifetime.

Kahlo, born in 1907 in a suburb of Mexico City, was greatly affected by two terrible events early in her life. At the age of seven, she suffered from polio.[2] The disease twisted her foot so that it
10 always pointed out, and caused her right leg to grow to a shorter length than her left leg. As a result, Kahlo's spine and pelvis became twisted as she grew older. Then, in 1925, while riding in a school bus, she was involved in a traffic accident, breaking her pelvis[3] and back in several places. Throughout the rest of her life, the artist **underwent** more than thirty operations on her spine and leg, but nothing was able cure the **severe** pain in her back and leg. However, the accident had an
15 unexpected side effect. It led Kahlo to begin painting. While lying in her bed recovering in her parents' home, Kahlo taught herself to paint and created her first self-portrait.

Despite the tragic events in her life, Kahlo had a reputation for **inspiring** excitement, happiness, and drama wherever she went. She often wore elaborate native jewelry and bright clothing, making her a highly visible student at school. She also **typically** wore her hair tied up on top of
20 her head with bright ribbons, in the style of the native people of Oaxaca, Mexico. Her preferred fashion and hairstyle are exhibited in the various self-portraits Kahlo painted.

Kahlo was not only an artist. She was also a political **activist** and an active member of the Young Communist League, an organization founded by another famous Mexican artist, Diego Rivera, who married Kahlo in 1929. In her early works Rivera's strong **influence** on Kahlo's style can be
25 seen, but her later works from the 1940s, known today as her best work, show less influence from her husband.

Kahlo's most famous works from the 1930s and 1940s did not attract much attention in the art world at that time, even in her home country of Mexico. Although her works were shown in exhibitions in New York and Paris in the 1930s, her first one-woman show in Mexico was not
30 held until 1953. At the time, Kahlo was suffering much pain and could not even get out of bed. But she was determined not to miss the opening night of her show, so she arranged for an ambulance to take her to the gallery. In the gallery, she lay all evening in a large bed where visitors could come and **congratulate** her.

Kahlo died in 1954 in her parents' home. The official report said that she died from a blood clot,[4]
35 but some people believe she might have **committed suicide** through an overdose[5] of painkillers. The final words in Kahlo's diary were, "I hope the exit is joyful—and I hope never to come back."

For more than a decade Kahlo's works remained unnoticed by the world at large, but in the 1970s her work began to develop an almost cult-like[6] following. Kahlo postcards, T-shirts, and buttons appeared, and several famous movie stars began collecting prints of her work. Various
40 documentary films on Kahlo and the Hollywood film *Frida* (2002), starring Mexican actress Salma Hayek, have helped spread the fame of one of Mexico's most important artists even further.

_____ **minutes** _____ **seconds** (649 words)

---

[1] **asbestos** a kind of mineral known for its resistance to fire
[2] **polio** a disease that attacks the spine and nerves and can cause paralysis
[3] **pelvis** the large bone in the hips
[4] **blood clot** a solid lump of blood in the body
[5] **overdose** too much of a drug. The prefix "over-" means "too much."
[6] **cult-like** a cult is an extreme religious group. The suffix "-like" means "seeming to be or typical."

Reading Comprehension

Circle the letter of the best answer.

1. What did the critic probably mean by calling Kahlo's paintings "a ribbon around a bomb"?

    a. They were paintings of bombs.

    b. She tied ribbons around her paintings.

    c. The expression was the title of a documentary.

    d. They were beautiful, but the subject was controversial.

2. Which sentence about Kahlo's life is NOT true?

    a. She was involved in politics.

    b. She is more famous today than during her life.

    c. She eventually recovered from her injuries.

    d. She stood out from other students in her school.

3. The passage mentions Kahlo's paintings of . . .

    a. her husband.   **b.** communists.   **c.** bombs.   **d.** herself.

4. Which sentence about Kahlo's first Mexican exhibition is true?

    a. She shared the exhibition with her husband.   **c.** It took place in the 1930s.

    b. She was unable to attend.   **d.** She spent the evening in bed.

5. According to the passage, Kahlo's best paintings were painted in the . . .

    a. 1920s.   **b.** 1930s.   **c.** 1940s.   **d.** 1950s.

Idioms

Find each idiom in the story.

1. **side effect**—*effects of a drug (apart from curing the illness) that are bad; an additional unplanned and unpleasant result of a situation*
    - You should ask the doctor if this medicine has any **side effects**.
    - One **side effect** of the new tax has been the loss of thousands of jobs.

2. **have an impact on**—*influence; affect*
    - In some countries, which elementary school you went to can **have an impact on** your career for the rest of your life.
    - My neighbor's cats have **had a** terrible **impact on** the birds in the area.

3. **be a big name**—*be successful or famous*
    - My uncle **is a big name** in the world of archaeology.
    - Since the success of her last movie, she **has become a big name** star.

Vocabulary Reinforcement

A. Circle the letter of the word or phrase that best completes the sentence.

1. His novel was _____ by his experiences in India when he was a child.

   a. inspired   **b.** undergone   **c.** congratulated   **d.** involved

2. There is a great film _____ in the newspaper, whose reviews I read every week.

   a. actor   **b.** director   **c.** critic   **d.** activist

3. Everyone _____ Kelly when she won the race.

   a. inspired   **b.** congratulated   **c.** influenced   **d.** had an impact on

4. The medicine eventually cured the disease, but the _____ were terrible.

   a. remedies   **b.** therapies   **c.** influences   **d.** side effects

5. The long rainy season _____ the number of tourists.

   a. had an impact on   **b.** appreciated   **c.** was worse off   **d.** had a tendency to

6. My cousin isn't a _____ elementary school student—she's already ready to take university entrance exams.

   a. severe   **b.** typical   **c.** practical   **d.** diplomatic

7. Young people are often easily _____ by their friends.

   a. congratulated   **b.** had an impact   **c.** influenced   **d.** committed

8. My friend recently had a blood clot and had to _____ surgery.

   a. commit   **b.** appreciate   **c.** sustain   **d.** undergo

B. Complete the passage with the correct form of items from the box. One item is extra.

undergo	severe	a big name	side effects	commit suicide	appreciate	an activist

Although Frida Kahlo is regarded as (1)_____ among Mexican artists today, her work was not widely (2)_____ during her lifetime. Kahlo started painting after suffering (3)_____ injuries in a car accident. Along with painting, Kahlo was also interested in politics, and was (4)_____ while she was a member of the Young Communist League. Although Kahlo (5)_____ surgery many times for her injuries, she remained in constant pain, and died in 1954, possibly by (6)_____.

What Do You Think?

1. What do you think of Frida Kahlo's painting on page 13? What artists do you like? Why do you like them?

2. Are there any famous people in your country who were more famous after their deaths than while they were alive? What do you know about them?

The History of English

T H E
Tragicall Hiſtorie of
H A M L E T,

Prince of Denmarke.

By William Shakeſpeare.

Newly imprinted and enlarged to almoſt as much
againe as it was, according to the true and perfect
Coppie.

AT LONDON,
Printed by I. R. for N. L. and are to be ſold at his
ſhoppe vnder Saint Dunſtons Church in
Fleeſtreet. 1605.

▊ Before You Read

Answer the following questions.

1. What do you know about the history of your own language?

   _____

   _____

2. When do you think people started speaking English? Where did the English language come from?

   _____

   _____

3. How many words do you think there are in the English language?

   _____

   _____

   _____

▊ Target Vocabulary

Match each word with the best meaning.

1. _F_ absorb
2. _b_ combine
3. _e_ conquer
4. _g_ dialect
5. _h_ linguist
6. _c_ revolution
7. _j_ settle
8. _a_ split
9. _d_ trace
10. _i_ usage

a. divide (v); a division (n)

b. join together

c. a big change, sometimes by war, in a government, economy, or field of study

d. follow something to its origin; track down (v); a sign that something or someone was in a place (n)

e. fight and take control of people or a place (in war)

f. take in (e.g., water into a sponge)

g. a regional variety of a language

h. a person who studies languages

i. the way something, e.g. a word, is used

j. move to and make a home in an area

Linguists trace the roots of English back to an ancient language spoken by tribes in Europe and Asia. This language today is known simply as Indo-European. As the speakers of this language moved to different areas, various **dialects** of the language began to develop. These dialects eventually developed into several groups: the Romance languages, including Greek, Latin, and

5　French, and the Germanic languages, including German, Swedish, Dutch, and English. Today, about 150 languages, with about three billion speakers, can trace their roots to Indo-European. A few words in each of these languages can be seen as evidence that they all came from the same root language. The English word *father*, for instance, came from the same Indo-European root word as the Latin word *pater*, the German word *vater*, and the Sanskrit word *pitr*.

10　Around 400 or 500 A.D., people from northern Europe began to **settle** in the country known today as England. These settlers spoke languages that were closely related to each other, so when they came to England they easily mixed their languages to create Old English. There were actually people already living in England at that time, the Celts, but the Europeans pushed the Celtic population north and west, into Scotland, Wales, and Ireland. Therefore, the Celtic language had

15　very little influence on Old English. Some Norse words, such as *get*, *wrong*, and *leg*, came into the English language when Vikings began to attack England from Scandinavia in the ninth century, but Old English did not change much at that time.

English underwent major changes after France **conquered** England in 1066. When the French leader, William the Conqueror, took control of England, his dialect of Old French became the

20　language of the kings and nobility in England. Evidence of this change in the language can still be found in English today. For example, lower-class cooks in an English castle prepared meat from *cows*, *pigs*, and *sheep*. But when this meat was served to the king, it was called *beef*, *pork*, and *mutton*. Both sets of words continue to be used to this day. In other cases, French words replaced Old English words completely, as in the case of *uncle* replacing *eam* and *firen* giving way to

25　*crime*. In addition, new words were created in English at this time by **combining** an Old English word with a French word, such as the French *gentle* combining with the Old English *man* to create *gentleman*. As all of the above changes took root in the language, Old English evolved into what is now known as Middle English.

The next step in the evolution of the English language, the step from Middle to Modern English,

30　occurred in the 1500s during the Renaissance. At this time, educated people were interested in learning and using Greek and Latin, so many words with Greek and Latin roots appeared in English at this time. This was also the period when Shakespeare made his personal impact on the English language. Through his writing, Shakespeare brought almost 2,000 words into common **usage**, including such words as *critical*, *majestic*, and *dwindle*. He also coined such common

35　phrases as "flesh and blood" and "vanish into thin air," which are still used to this day.

BIOLOGICAL ← ⟶ SIT FOR SURE ⟶ fallen in sleep

But English did not stop evolving with Shakespeare. The Industrial **Revolution** and the settling of English speakers in the United States both brought about further changes in the language. With technological advances, new words were created from Greek and Latin roots (*oxygen* and *vaccine*) as well as from combining existing English words (*horsepower* and *airplane*). And as

40　English speakers in North America separated themselves from English speakers in Britain, the language further **split** into different **dialects** in each country.

Even today, English continues to **absorb** new words into its vocabulary. Take for example the following list of common words borrowed from other languages that most English speakers probably don't even recognize as foreign at all: *shampoo* (Hindi), *sauna* (Finnish), *tycoon*

45　(Japanese), *canyon* (Spanish), *coffee* (Arabic), and *ketchup* or *catsup* (Chinese). English today has a larger vocabulary than any other language—the latest edition of the *Oxford English Dictionary* contains over 230,000 unique words.

_____ **minutes** _____ **seconds** (687 words)

Reading Comprehension

Circle the letter of the best answer.

1. According to the passage, the fact that the German and Latin words for *father* are similar means . . .

   a. Latin evolved from German.

   b. German evolved from Latin.

   c. both languages evolved from an earlier language.

   d. nothing. It's just by chance.

2. Which of these is NOT mentioned in the passage as a way of creating new English words?

   a. word combining

   b. importing from other languages

   c. coining new words from foreign roots

   d. creation of words by dictionary authors

3. According to the passage, which of these languages has had the least influence on English?

   a. Celtic   **b.** Norse   **c.** French   **d.** Latin

4. Which of these languages was not brought to England by an invading force?

   a. Old English   **b.** French   **c.** Greek   **d.** Norse

5. Where do most of the new words in English today come from?

   a. other dialects

   b. North America

   c. the *Oxford English Dictionary*

   d. The passage doesn't say.

Idioms

Find each idiom in the story.

1. **take root**—*become established*
   - Environmental activism didn't really **take root** until around 1970.
   - Communism never really **took root** in that country.

2. **(vanish) into/(appear) out of thin air**—*(vanish/appear) suddenly and from (or to) nowhere*
   - The flight landed safely, but my luggage has disappeared **into thin air**.
   - She's great at coming up with new ideas **out of thin air**.

3. **coin a (phrase/word)**—*start a new phrase or expression*
   - The **word** "cyberspace" **was coined** by the science fiction writer William Gibson in 1984.
   - I wonder who first **coined the expression**, "It's raining cats and dogs."

Vocabulary Reinforcement

A. Circle the letter of the word or phrase that best completes the sentence.

1. My aunt, the _____, is particularly interested in Asian languages.
   a. linguist **b.** critic **c.** conqueror **d.** activist

2. The new system of government quickly _____ in the society.
   a. split **b.** combined **c.** took root **d.** settled

3. The end of the eighteenth century was an interesting time, with the American and French _____ happening around the same time.
   a. governments **b.** revolutions **c.** conquerors **d.** policies

4. My grandparents _____ in Australia over eighty years ago.
   a. traced **b.** absorbed **c.** underwent **d.** settled

5. Have you seen my keys? They've _____.
   a. scratched the surface **c.** vanished into thin air
   b. taken root **d.** seen the big picture

6. The teacher explained the _____ of the word to the class.
   a. big picture **b.** linguist **c.** usage **d.** vocabulary

7. I hope you _____ all the hard work I've done for you.
   a. congratulate **b.** appreciate **c.** trace **d.** absorb

8. In 1993, Czechoslovakia _____ into two countries, the Czech Republic and Slovakia.
   a. split **b.** absorbed **c.** revolted **d.** conquered

B. Complete the passage with the correct form of items from the box. One item is extra.

absorb	coin	combine	conquer	dialect	take root	trace

Linguists have (1)_____ the origin of English back to a language known simply as Indo-European. This ancient language split into (2)_____ that became various European languages. People speaking these different, but related, languages (3)_____ their languages when they lived together in England. Later, French heavily influenced English when French speakers (4)_____ the people living in England. Then, during the Renaissance, Shakespeare (5)_____ many words and phrases commonly used in English. Today, English continues to (6)_____ words from languages around the world.

What Do You Think?

1. Do you think that it is necessary for English to have so many words? How many words do you think your language has?

2. Why do you think that English has become so commonly used internationally? What are the pros and cons of having English as an international language?

The Tiger in the Living Room

Before You Read

Answer the following questions.

1. Are cats a common pet in your country? Have you ever had a pet cat?

_____

2. What are some of the advantages and disadvantages of having a cat rather than other types of pet?

_____

3. How long do you think people have been keeping cats as pets?

_____

Target Vocabulary

Match each word with the best meaning.

1. _____ accuse
2. _____ analyze
3. _____ device
4. _____ domesticate
5. _____ drown
6. _____ era
7. _____ mourn
8. _____ myth
9. _____ spokesperson
10. _____ wrap

a. to charge someone with a crime or doing something wrong

b. a person who communicates the ideas and opinions of another person, group, or company

c. to cover something with material that surrounds it

d. an electrical or mechanical machine or tool

e. a period of history with a particular characteristic or quality

f. a legend

g. die from being kept underwater and unable to breathe

h. to examine something to understand what it means

i. to tame (an animal that was once wild)

j. to feel sad at the death of someone

21

It seems that there is no middle ground when it comes to cats. People either love them or hate them. These feelings are not new either. All through history, cats have been worshiped or hated. A study of ancient writings and evidence found in tombs indicates that for the past 5,000 years, cats have been kept as pets in China, Arabia, Egypt, and India. However, this isn't very long compared
5 to dogs, which have been domesticated for 50,000 years. Still, while the period in which cats have been **domesticated** may be quite short, it has definitely had its high and low points.

Cats were at their highest position of domesticated life in ancient Egypt. There were more cats living in Egypt during the time of the pharaohs than in any other place in the world since that time. This high number of cats was probably due to the laws protecting them. Cats were associated
10 with the moon goddess, Bast, so the Egyptians worshiped them as holy animals. If anyone was caught killing a cat, the person could be put to death. Families in Egypt also **mourned** the death of a cat and had the body of the dead cat **wrapped** in cloth before it was finally laid to rest. This respect for cats carried over to the Roman Empire where cats were the only animals allowed into temples. This fact was probably due to the ability of cats to keep the temples free of mice and rats.

15 With the coming of the Dark Ages[1] in Europe, the place of cats in society took a turn for the worse. Because they were associated so closely with the "old religions" of Egypt and the Roman Empire, Christians began to associate cats with pagan[2] beliefs. Cats had a reputation as helpers of witches. When a person was **accused** of being a witch, a cat would often be put on trial with the person. The cat would be tortured[3] to try and make the person tell the truth, and usually the cat
20 and the person would end up being burned in a bonfire or **drowned**. Bonfires of collected cats were not uncommon during this time.

The days of hunting witches have ended, but other **myths** about cats still hold out. For a while, people in some places used to bury live cats under new buildings for good luck. As well, many people today continue to believe that black cats bring bad luck. If a black cat walks in front of a
25 person, that person must take extra care in the near future to watch out for dangerous situations. Regardless of superstition, cats remain a popular pet today. Some cat experts believe that a cat can never truly be domesticated because it may turn wild and run away at any time. However, this claim has not put people off keeping cats in their homes. A third of homes in the United States have cats, and one out of every three of these homes keeps both a dog and a cat. Especially in large
30 cities, many people in small apartments have found that cats make much better pets than dogs.

Cats may not be worshiped as gods any more, but there are people who seem to think of their cats as their children. These cat owners will do almost anything to keep their pets healthy and happy. For those cat owners who have always wondered what their pets are trying to tell them, a Japanese company may have come up with the perfect invention. In 2003, the Takara Company announced
35 the Meowlingual, a cat translation **device**. The Meowlingual uses a microphone, display, and cat voice **analyzer** to analyze a cat's meows[4] to determine which of 200 phrases a cat is trying to say.

According to a company **spokesperson**, ". . . cat owners all over the world have been telling Takara, 'We want a cat translator!'" Now, the company "is making their dream come true by bringing in a new **era** of communication between cat lovers and their pets."

 _____ **minutes** _____ **seconds** (673 words)

---

[1] **the Dark Ages** the period between the end of the Roman Empire and the Renaissance (approximately the fifth century to the fourteenth century)
[2] **pagan** someone who doesn't believe in any of the world's major religions, and who usually worships nature
[3] **torture** cause pain to a person for punishment, or to get information
[4] **meow** the noise a cat makes

Reading Comprehension

Circle the letter of the best answer.

1. Which of these is NOT discussed in the passage?
   - **a.** the status of cats throughout history
   - **b.** the evolution of different species of cats
   - **c.** the popularity of cats today
   - **d.** communication between cats and their owners

2. The second paragraph describes . . .
   - **a.** how Bast became a goddess.
   - **b.** the low point in the history of cats.
   - **c.** the high point in the history of cats.
   - **d.** the reason why cats are such good hunters.

3. How were cats treated in Europe during the Dark Ages?
   - **a.** as farm animals
   - **b.** as food
   - **c.** as magical creatures
   - **d.** as honored guests

4. The fifth paragraph describes theories of how cats . . .
   - **a.** became the enemy of dogs.
   - **b.** can be good or bad luck.
   - **c.** cannot be trained.
   - **d.** protect people.

5. According to the passage, what percentage of people in the United States keep both a cat and a dog?
   - **a.** about 10 percent
   - **b.** nearly 25 percent
   - **c.** about 33 percent
   - **d.** close to 50 percent

Idioms

Find each idiom in the story.

1. **take a turn for the worse**—*go from good to bad*
   - My grandfather's health **took a turn for the worse** last winter.
   - I hope nothing happens to make the situation **take a turn for the worse**.

2. **hold out**—*continue after others stop or finish*
   - Mary was the only member of the committee to **hold out** on the decision.
   - Some animals are in danger of dying out, but a few survivors are **holding out**.

3. **put (someone) off (something)**—*make someone dislike someone, or not want to do something*
   - Arnold was going to buy a new car, but the price **put him off**.
   - The last hamburger I ate made me sick, and it's really **put me off** them.

Vocabulary Reinforcement

A. Circle the letter of the word or phrase that best completes the sentence.

1. The new tax plan was announced by a government _____.
   a. activist   **b.** president   **c.** linguist   **d.** spokesperson

2. Could you please _____ this for me? It's a gift.
   a. wrap   **b.** analyze   **c.** receive   **d.** accuse

3. For many older people, the 1960s is still their favorite _____.
   a. year   **b.** era   **c.** device   **d.** status

4. Some people think there is a monster in Loch Ness in Scotland, but others think it is just _____.
   a. a myth   **b.** a device   **c.** severe   **d.** doubt

5. Rika told her friends so many bad things about the restaurant she really ___.
   a. had an impact on them   **c.** put them off
   b. coined a phrase   **d.** took a turn for the worse

6. This _____ is used for removing the pits from olives.
   a. evidence   **b.** device   **c.** dialect   **d.** therapy

7. This test is used to _____ a person's personality.
   a. analyze   **b.** wrap   **c.** domesticate   **d.** combine

8. Over 500 people _____ when the boat sank.
   a. committed suicide   **b.** drowned   **c.** mourned   **d.** accused

B. Complete the passage with the correct form of items from the box. One item is extra.

accuse	analyze	domesticate	drown	hold out	mourn	take a turn for the worse

Writings and pictures indicate that cats have been (1)_____ for around 5,000 years. Over this time, cats have been both worshiped and hated. In ancient Egypt, when a cat died, people (2)_____ it in a special ritual. However, during the Dark Ages, the status of cats (3)_____. They were put on trial with people (4)_____ of being witches. Often they were burned or (5)_____ with the person on trial. Today, cats are treated better, but some myths about them (6)_____ to this day.

What Do You Think?

1. What do you think of the idea of the Meowlingual device? Would you be interested in it? Are there any other animals you would like to be able to understand?

2. Are there any superstitions about animals in your country? Which animals are regarded as either lucky or unlucky? Do you agree with these beliefs?

Review

A. Circle the correct answer for each question.

1. Which would most people prefer was sustained? **a.** peace   **b.** a war
2. For which job do you need to be more ambitious? **a.** president   **b.** fitness instructor
3. For which are you more likely to be appreciated? **a.** doing a bad thing   **b.** doing a good thing
4. Where is a person more likely to settle? **a.** a new country   **b.** a hospital
5. Which of these is an activist more likely to be interested in? **a.** business success   **b.** political issues
6. Which of these is better for wrapping things in? **a.** paper   **b.** wood
7. Who are you more likely to mourn? **a.** a new baby   **b.** a dead person
8. Which would more people go along with? **a.** a bad idea   **b.** a good idea
9. How do most people feel about doing something they really enjoy? **a.** enthusiastic   **b.** resistant
10. Which of these animals is more domesticated? **a.** a tiger   **b.** a sheep

B. Complete the paragraph with the correct form of items from the box. Two items are extra.

| better off | dialect | doubt | endangered | linguist | policy |
| resist | severe | side effect | sustain | tend to be | trace |

How many languages exist in the world today? It's difficult to know exactly, but most
(1)_____ generally agree that there are probably about 6,800 unique languages spoken in
the world today, as well as a number of (2)_____. Unfortunately, many of these languages
are (3)_____, and many scientists (4)_____ that more than half of them will
survive until the end of this century.

There are many reasons why a language may die out, but one thing endangered languages all have in
common is that they are spoken by a minority of people in that country, and then usually as a second
language. Also, for many reasons, parents don't pass these languages on to their children, so there are
too few speakers to (5)_____ the language. Some of the languages in (6)_____
danger of disappearing have only one living speaker. Often a language becomes endangered as a result
of government (7)_____, which made speaking the endangered language illegal.

Some people think that it doesn't matter if languages completely disappear. They think that the world
would be (8)_____ if everyone spoke the same language. However, the problem is that as
languages die, there is a(n) (9)_____ that the culture that is tied to that language
(10)_____ affected as well.

C. Circle the odd one out in each group.

1. **a.** revolution   **b.** therapy   **c.** remedy   **d.** treatment
2. **a.** influence   **b.** impact   **c.** trace   **d.** effect
3. **a.** drown   **b.** fly   **c.** sink   **d.** float
4. **a.** device   **b.** policy   **c.** strategy   **d.** plan
5. **a.** superstition   **b.** myth   **c.** event   **d.** legend
6. **a.** era   **b.** period   **c.** century   **d.** custom
7. **a.** global   **b.** specific   **c.** worldwide   **d.** universal
8. **a.** congratulate   **b.** appreciate   **c.** accuse   **d.** thank
9. **a.** dialect   **b.** harvest   **c.** linguist   **d.** phrase
10. **a.** undergo   **b.** conquer   **c.** invade   **d.** take over

D. Use the clues below to complete the crossword.

Across

1. To talk to angry people without upsetting them, you need to be _____.
6. The invention of color television put an end to the _____ of black-and-white TV.
7. a person who reviews movies, books, restaurants, etc. for a newspaper
8. die from being underwater and unable to breathe
9. An impatient person finds it difficult to _____ late people. (3 words)
14. This new sponge is able to _____ a lot of water.
15. a variety of a language spoken in a particular region
16. the way something is used
17. common, usual, normal

Down

1. You need to be _____ to catch crocodiles.
2. The company's new _____ bans smoking in the office.
3. a legend or old story
4. Over two hundred years ago, Europeans moved to Australia, and a new society _____.
5. mix; join together
7. take over another country
10. She comes from a very old family. You can _____ her relatives back to the twelfth century.

11. It would be nice if everyone in the company had their own office, but it's just not _____.
12. For some people palm reading is a way to gain _____ into a person's personality.
13. To make Australian wine you need to _____ grapes at the end of January.
15. to think that something is probably not true

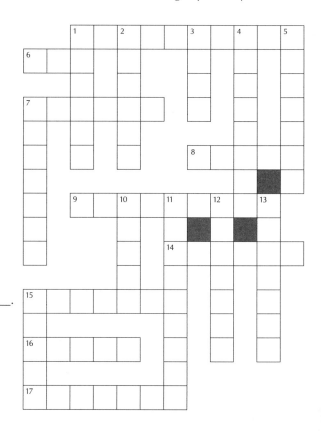

The Mid-Autumn Festival

Before You Read

Answer the following questions.

1. What are some of the big festivals in your country? What do people do at this time?

   _____

   _____

   _____

2. Is there any time of year in your country when families come together to celebrate?

   _____

   _____

   _____

3. Does your country have any kind of autumn festival? If yes, what do people do then?

   _____

   _____

   _____

Target Vocabulary

Match each word with the best meaning.

1. _____ commemorate
2. _____ gaze
3. _____ glow
4. _____ lunar
5. _____ potion
6. _____ precise
7. _____ sacrifice
8. _____ scholar
9. _____ tutor
10. _____ uprising

a. loss or giving up of something valuable for a specific purpose

b. to celebrate the memory of someone or some event

c. give off a soft light

d. exact; accurate

e. a person of great learning, usually in a particular subject

f. a teacher who helps students individually with other courses (n); to help a student with a course (v)

g. a revolution

h. to look steadily at something for a long time

i. relating to the moon

j. strong liquid medicine, often with magical properties

Without question, one of the most important festivals in many Asian countries is the Mid-Autumn Festival, also known as the Moon Festival. As the name suggests, this festival is held in the middle of autumn every year. Because the **precise** date of the Mid-Autumn Festival is based on the Chinese **lunar** calendar, it is held on a different date every year, but it is always on the
5   fifteenth day of the eighth lunar month. This date usually falls sometime in late August or September.

There are many legends about the origins of this festival. One ancient Chinese myth tells of a great archer, Hou Yi, and his wife, Chang O (or Chang'e). According to the legend, at one time there were ten suns in the sky, rather than the one we have today, and the world was in danger of
10 dying. Hou Yi used his bow to shoot nine of the suns, and save the earth. As a reward, the Goddess of the Western Heaven gave Hou Yi the elixir of immortality.[1] However, the curious Chang O drank it accidentally. She found herself becoming lighter and lighter until eventually she reached the moon, where she lives in her palace to this day, with a rabbit who makes magic **potions** for the gods.

15 In China as well as in other countries, this festival is marked by family reunions, **gazing** at the moon, and by friends and family exchanging "moon cakes." The moon cake is a small round cake, stuffed with such things as red bean paste, five different types of nuts, lotus paste, and the yolk from a duck egg. The history of moon cakes traditionally goes back to the fourteenth century, when China was ruled by the Mongols of the Yuan Dynasty. According to legend, an
20 **uprising** against the Mongols was planned, and details were written on secret messages that were hidden inside round cakes. The message said that the uprising would start on the fifteenth day of the eighth month. The uprising was successful, and to this day, the event is **commemorated** with moon cakes. In China today, moon cakes are an important part of the festival, and they are passed out to family members, employers, and friends. In the old days, **scholars** who **tutored**
25 students also gave moon cakes to each of their students, who then gave their tutors an envelope of money.

In Hong Kong during the Mid-Autumn Festival, a table is set outside the house, with dishes of round fruit (which represent the full moon), moon cakes, rice, wine, and tea. Today, most families in Hong Kong celebrate this holiday with a family dinner. If there are young children in the
30 family, parents may take them out to a nearby park or to the beach so that everyone can gaze at the full moon. The family may also set up lit candles all around themselves while they watch the moon rise.

Korea also celebrates its own version of the Mid-Autumn Festival. All stores and businesses take the day off so that families can spend the day together. On the morning of this holiday, almost
35 everyone dresses up in their finest clothes—men in suits and women in the national dress of Korea. For many people, the first business of the day is to visit the family burial place where families offer **sacrifices** of traditional food at graves. The family then comes together for dinner.

The Mid-Autumn Festival in Vietnam is seen as a children's festival, but it is also enjoyed by adults. Moon cakes are exchanged and enjoyed by everyone. Paper lanterns are also an important
40 part of the celebration in Vietnam. Many shops begin selling the lanterns long before the festival, and children may be seen playing with them for several days before the actual day of the celebration. On the night of the Mid-Autumn Festival, children put candles into their lanterns, and then they all take their lanterns out onto the streets where the colorful parade of **glowing** shapes lights up the night under the full moon.

 _____ **minutes** _____ **seconds** (673 words)

---

[1] **elixir of immortality** a potion that enables the drinker to live forever

Reading Comprehension

Circle the letter of the best answer.

1. What is the best title for this passage?
   - **a.** The History of Moon Cakes
   - **b.** Famous Chinese Festivals
   - **c.** Celebrating the Moon Festival
   - **d.** Origins of the Lunar Calendar

2. When is the Moon Festival held?
   - **a.** August 15th
   - **b.** the beginning of autumn
   - **c.** It changes every year.
   - **d.** every September

3. The passage does NOT mention moon cakes in which place?
   - **a.** China
   - **b.** Hong Kong
   - **c.** Korea
   - **d.** Vietnam

4. According to the legend mentioned in the passage, which of these statements is NOT true?
   - **a.** Chang O and Hou Yi live on the moon.
   - **b.** The gods take potions from a rabbit.
   - **c.** The rabbit lives in a palace.
   - **d.** At one time there were more suns than today.

5. Which of these statements about the Mid-Autumn Festival in Vietnam is true?
   - **a.** Children traditionally use candles to burn their lanterns.
   - **b.** The parade is held during the daytime.
   - **c.** Lanterns can be bought in advance of the parade.
   - **d.** Only children exchange moon cakes.

Idioms

Find each idiom in the story.

1. **pass out**—*give to many people; hand out*
   - Matthew **passed out** a survey to all the people at the meeting.
   - The teacher **passed out** the new textbooks at the start of the lesson.

2. **dress up/get dressed up**—*put on nice or formal clothes*
   - Why is Ellen so **dressed up**? Does she have a date?
   - You don't need to **dress up** for the party. It's casual.

3. **take the day off**—*not go to work for personal reasons*
   - Mary hasn't **taken a day off** in over three years.
   - I'm going to **take the day off** on Friday so I can go to the doctor.

Vocabulary Reinforcement

A. Circle the letter of the word or phrase that best completes the sentence.

1. In order to save the patient with cancer, doctors had to _____ his leg.

   a. commemorate   **b.** split   **c.** sacrifice   **d.** put off

2. There are over two hundred _____ conducting research at that university.

   a. scholars   **b.** tutors   **c.** activists   **d.** courses

3. Alice drank a magic _____ that made her smaller than a mouse.

   a. remedy   **b.** potion   **c.** therapy   **d.** uprising

4. The _____ number of students at that school is 2,143.

   a. approximate   **b.** general   **c.** precise   **d.** lunar

5. The French Revolution began as a(n) _____ against the King in 1789.

   a. sacrifice   **b.** activist   **c.** conquering   **d.** uprising

6. To help me pass the exam, I decided to hire a math _____.

   a. tutor   **b.** scholar   **c.** critic   **d.** device

7. There was a huge party to _____ the 500th anniversary of the founding of the town.

   a. domesticate   **b.** appreciate   **c.** commemorate   **d.** pass out

8. What a beautiful painting. I could _____ at it for hours.

   a. watch   **b.** gaze   **c.** appreciate   **d.** glow

B. Complete the passage with the correct form of items from the box. One item is extra.

commemorate	take the day off	dress up	precise	lunar	glow	pass out

The Mid-Autumn Festival is an important celebration throughout Asia. Because the date for this festival is set according to the (1)_____ calendar, using the moon rather than the sun, the (2)_____ date varies from year to year. A common element of this festival shared by many Asian countries is the tradition of eating moon cakes, which are (3)_____ to family and friends. In some countries, people (4)_____ so they can spend it together with their family. Family members may (5)_____ in nice clothes for the occasion, but they typically enjoy a meal together. Then some families go outside to gaze at the (6)_____ of the full moon.

What Do You Think?

1. Do you know the background, or any legends, surrounding other celebrations?

2. If you could create a new national holiday, when would it be? What would it celebrate? What would people do on that day?

Car Culture

Before You Read

Answer the following questions.

1. How many cars do you think there are in the world? How about in your country?

_____

2. In what ways do you think cars have changed the ways people live?

_____

3. Would you say that cars are an important part of the culture of your country?

_____

Target Vocabulary

Match each word with the best meaning.

1. _____ behavior
2. _____ boom
3. _____ commute
4. _____ conservative
5. _____ fatal
6. _____ isolated
7. _____ outrageous
8. _____ prior (to)
9. _____ rural
10. _____ transform

a. a way of doing and saying things

b. slow to change; careful; in favor of keeping the old way of doing things

c. to grow rapidly (an economy or an industry)

d. before

e. relating to the country rather than the city

f. to change from one shape or appearance to another

g. to travel to and from work or school regularly

h. causing death

i. separated from others; alone

j. shocking

Worldwide, 40 million new passenger cars are built every year. A recent study estimates that the number of cars on the world's roads will triple over the next twenty years—to 1.5 billion cars. Most of this growth will take place in China, where there is currently one car for every hundred people. In comparison, a survey done in 2003 revealed that there were more cars in the United
5　States than drivers. The United States, possibly more than any other country, has been completely **transformed** by cars.

Cars are so common today that it is difficult to imagine a time without them. However, cars did not become necessities for families in the United States until after World War II. **Prior to** that time, cars were seen mainly as toys for the rich. By the end of the war, however, people were tired of
10　saving their money and rationing items. They were ready to have some fun. Unlike Europe and Japan, whose industries had been wiped out by World War II, factories in the United States could quickly be changed from production of wartime items to mass production of such luxury items as cars. Two other factors also helped the population of the United States take cars into their lives— low oil prices and drivable roads.

15　As cars grew in popularity in the United States, there were also changes in lifestyle. Farmers who were once **isolated** from society by **rural** life now took weekend trips into the city. Also, workers in the cities no longer needed to live in inner-city housing in order to keep their jobs at nearby factories. Those who made enough money moved out of the cities and into the suburbs. Now that each family had its own car, **commuting** to work from the suburbs became a common practice.
20　The car **boom** also brought about changes in many businesses. Suddenly, drive-in movie theaters[1] and drive-thru restaurants[2] began to appear across the country.

Cars not only changed the way people lived, they also changed the way they thought. Traditionally, because young people spent most of their time outside school in and around the home, the strongest role models for teenagers were their parents. However, once they had their
25　own driver's license and had access to cars, teens began spending more time out "cruising" with friends. Therefore, they became less likely to follow the **behavior** of their parents and more likely to follow the behavior of their friends. The word "cruising" was coined to refer to the act of driving with the purpose of watching others while being seen. One city in California, Van Nuys, was particularly famous for the nightly ritual of cruising. It was not uncommon for people who
30　lived 300 kilometers away to drive to Van Nuys and drive up and down Van Nuys Boulevard along with hundreds of other teenagers cruising the street. People who lived along the street would sit on the porch in front of their houses to watch the parade of cars slowly drive by each night.

The car boom of the 1950s continued into the 1960s as new car models became more and more **outrageous**. In the early days of cars, car design was quite **conservative**. Henry Ford, founder of
35　the Ford Motor Company, is claimed to have said about his most popular car of the 1920s, the Model T, "You can have it in any color, as long as it's black." All at once, huge tail fins, super-powered engines, and multicolored bodies were only a few of the accessories new car buyers could choose from.

One thing producers paid little attention to, however, was safety. It wasn't until the mid-1960s that
40　consumers began to demand that all car companies include at least a few common safety features in new cars. These new standards eventually led to safety features such as seat belts, air bags, anti-lock brakes, and automatic door locks. Despite these safety features, there are over 1,250,000 **fatal** accidents involving cars, and 10–15 million injuries, worldwide every year.

_____ **minutes** _____ **seconds** (669 words)

---

[1] **drive-in movie theater** a cinema in which the customers sit in their own cars to watch the movie
[2] **drive-thru restaurant** a restaurant in which customers can buy food and take it away without leaving their cars

Reading Comprehension

Circle the letter of the best answer.

1. According to the recent study, approximately how many cars are there in the world today?

   a. 40 million   **b.** 500 million   **c.** 1.5 billion   **d.** 4.5 billion

2. According to the passage, what is one reason why cars didn't take off as quickly in Europe as in the United States?

   a. People weren't as interested in fun.   **c.** People couldn't afford cars.

   b. Fewer factories were able to make cars.   **d.** Fewer people lived on farms.

3. According to the passage, what was the greatest benefit of cars to American life?

   a. They provided people with more freedom to travel.

   b. They encouraged people to commute to and from work.

   c. They led to the development of drive-in movies and drive-thru restaurants.

   d. They allowed teenagers to spend more time with their friends.

4. The main point of the fourth paragraph is that cars . . .

   a. caused families to grow closer.

   b. changed the lives of teenagers.

   c. changed the lives of people living in Van Nuys.

   d. made cruising a popular activity.

5. Which colors was the Model T available in?

   a. any color   **c.** only conservative colors

   b. black   **d.** The passage doesn't say.

Idioms

Find each idiom in the story.

1. **as long as**—*only if*
   - I'll come to the party **as long as** Jeffrey does too.
   - You can borrow my car **as long as** you promise to drive carefully.

2. **bring about**—*cause to happen*
   - What **brought about** this change in your decision?
   - The results of the experiment **brought about** a new way of teaching.

3. **pay attention to**—*focus attention on; look and listen carefully*
   - Please **pay attention to** the television screen on your left.
   - The children refused to **pay attention to** their parents.

Vocabulary Reinforcement

A. Circle the letter of the word or phrase that best completes the sentence.

1. The class will meet two more times _____ the exam.
   a. as long as   b. since   c. along with   d. prior to

2. The dinner party tonight will be very formal, so please dress _____.
   a. outrageously   b. conservatively   c. controversially   d. ambitiously

3. There has been a tendency over the last century for many countries to be transformed from _____ societies to urban ones.
   a. rural   b. conservative   c. isolated   d. domesticated

4. She was awarded the Nobel Peace Prize for her work to _____ peace.
   a. transform   b. pay attention to   c. commute   d. bring about

5. I really enjoy weddings, _____ I don't have to make a speech!
   a. unless   b. as long as   c. despite   d. prior to

6. If you don't _____ the teacher, you won't learn anything.
   a. pass out   b. gaze   c. pay attention to   d. hold out

7. I wanted to buy a dress from that store, but the prices were _____.
   a. conservative   b. glowing   c. isolated   d. outrageous

8. Be careful with this medicine. If you drink too much it can be _____.
   a. a potion   b. typical   c. lunar   d. fatal

B. Complete the passage with the correct form of items from the box. One item is extra.

isolated	fatal	behavior	pay attention to	boom	commute	transform

As private passenger cars become more popular worldwide, the culture and (1)_____ of people will no doubt change. This can certainly be seen through the ways cars have (2)_____ American life and culture since 1945. Because people became able to (3)_____ to and from work by car, more families moved out of cities into the suburbs. In addition, farmers in (4)_____ areas could drive into cities more regularly. Worldwide, the last fifty years has seen a(n) (5)_____ in the number of cars. Unfortunately, one of the side effects of this increase in the number of cars has been a rise in the number of (6)_____ accidents.

What Do You Think?

1. Do you think that cars are a necessity or a luxury? Why?

2. Should young people have their own cars? Why or why not? How old should someone be before getting a car?

The Temple of Borobudur

Before You Read

Answer the following questions.

1. Where is Java? What do you know about it?

_____

2. What is the largest religious building that you have seen? Where was it?

_____

3. Do you know of any old buildings in your country that has been restored?

_____

Target Vocabulary

Match each word with the best meaning.

1. _____ erupt   **a.** person in charge of a state or region

2. _____ governor   **b.** huge; great

3. _____ ignorance   **c.** guard; protect from harm or change; keep in good condition

4. _____ interfere   **d.** legend; story

5. _____ magnificent   **e.** (for a volcano) to release lava, smoke, and ash

6. _____ massive   **f.** lack of education; lack of knowledge

7. _____ preserve   **g.** become involved in a situation where it doesn't concern you, and you are not welcome

8. _____ priceless

9. _____ tale   **h.** very beautiful or impressive

10. _____ well-meaning   **i.** intending to be helpful or kind, but unsuccessful or unhelpful

                            j. so valuable that no price would be enough

In 1814, England's lieutenant **governor** of the Indonesian island of Java, Thomas Stamford Raffles, sent a group of his men to look for a "mountain of Buddhist sculpture in stone" that was said to be buried in the jungle. Working from the **tales** of the local people, Mr. Raffles set his men to work digging at one of the many hills in central Java. Two months later, one of the men
5   working on the hill found a **magnificent** sculpture of Buddha carved in stone. The extraordinary temple of Borobudur, the largest Buddhist temple in the world, had been uncovered.

Construction of the temple had begun around 800 A.D. under the Sailendra Dynasty of Java. The temple was planned to be a symbolic representation of the universe and was built over a small hill. When seen from above, a person can easily make out the overall design of the temple. The
10   temple has ten levels, which represent the ten spiritual stages in the life of a Buddhist pilgrim as he or she travels from **ignorance** to Nirvana, the state of spiritual perfection or enlightenment.[1] The lower levels are shaped like squares to represent the stage of the journey where the pilgrim prepares him- or herself for enlightenment. The upper levels are circular, symbolizing the enlightenment of the pilgrim. The highest point of the temple is a stupa or shrine that rises to a
15   height of more than 35 meters. This marks the final point of the pilgrim's journey. Along the six-kilometer journey through all of the walkways of the temple leading up to the highest level, hundreds of carved images of the Buddha may be found.

After the temple was completed, it became the center of Buddhist worship in the Sailendra Kingdom until 930 A.D. In that year, the nearby volcano, Mount Merapi, **erupted**. Tons of ash
20   and lava covered Borobudur. Overnight, the temple disappeared. It was totally covered under layers of ash from the volcano.

The temple remained hidden until Mr. Raffles and his men uncovered it again in the 1800s. However, after Mr. Raffles left Java, work on the temple was carried on without much interest. Collectors of ancient artifacts stole **priceless** treasures from the temple, and soon, all work on
25   the temple came to a standstill. People living in the area began using stones from the temple to build and repair their homes. Additionally, **well-meaning** but mistaken Europeans, in an attempt to **preserve** the temple, cleared away the vegetation that covered it. Without realizing it, by removing the plants they had also removed the temple's protection from the weather. Over the following decades, Borobudur suffered more damage from wind and rain than in the preceding
30   thousand years.

In 1900, with Java under Dutch[2] control, an engineer named Dr. Theodore Van Erp was assigned the job of saving and rebuilding the temple. However, two world wars and a limited supply of money **interfered** with his work. In 1973, the United Nations Educational, Scientific, and Cultural Organization (UNESCO) stepped in and began the Borobudur Restoration Project. The project
35   had its work cut out for it in fully restoring the temple to its original state. The restoration took ten years and involved experts from twenty-seven countries. In total, over a million stones were moved, cleaned, and replaced. The restoration work was compared to completing a **massive** jigsaw puzzle.

When the thousand-year-old temple was finally reopened, the President of Indonesia said that
40   through the use of modern technology, "Borobudur will live a thousand years more." In 1991, Borobudur was placed on the UNESCO World Heritage list.

 _____ **minutes** _____ **seconds** (594 words)

---

[1] **enlightenment** (in Buddhist philosophy) a state in which there is no suffering or desire
[2] **Dutch** from the Netherlands

Reading Comprehension

Circle the letter of the best answer.

1. How did Thomas Raffles hear about the temple?

   a. His men told him.

   b. England told him.

   c. Javanese people told him.

   d. He found it himself.

2. What Buddhist idea is the design of the temple based on?

   a. nature

   b. the journey of pilgrims

   c. traditional Buddhist temples

   d. the universe

3. What would a pilgrim to the temple find at the end of his or her journey?

   a. a square platform

   b. a shrine

   c. a sculpture of Buddha

   d. a volcano

4. When Dr. Theodore Van Erp started his reconstruction work, which country controlled the temple?

   a. England   **b.** the Netherlands   **c.** Indonesia   **d.** Sailendra

5. Who did the most to restore the temple?

   a. Thomas Raffles

   b. Dr. Theodore Van Erp

   c. UNESCO

   d. European collectors

Idioms

Find each idiom in the story.

1. **have (your) work cut out for (you)**—*be in a difficult situation; have hard work ahead*
   - If you take that class, you'll really **have your work cut out for you**.
   - Emily **had her work cut out for her**. She was trying to start her law career as well as raise two children.

2. **make out**—*see, recognize*
   - Jennifer's so tall. It's always easy to **make her out** in a crowd.
   - I can't **make out** that sign. What does it say?

3. **come to a standstill**—*stop completely*
   - The project **came to a standstill** when the manager left the company.
   - Traffic usually **comes to a standstill** at around 5 P.M.

Vocabulary Reinforcement

A. Circle the letter of the word or phrase that best completes the sentence.

1. A _____ stone rolled down the mountain and crushed the house.
   a. magnificent   **b.** priceless   **c.** massive   **d.** well-meaning

2. It was difficult to _____ what the sign said from so far away.
   a. make out   **b.** pay attention to   **c.** bring about   **d.** erupt

3. As a rule, _____ of the law is no defense in court.
   a. interference   **b.** ignorance   **c.** sacrifice   **d.** accusation

4. In 2003, actor Arnold Schwarzenegger became _____ of California.
   a. lieutenant   **b.** scholar   **c.** spokesperson   **d.** governor

5. The zoo had to put up signs to stop _____ visitors from feeding the animals.
   a. interfering   **b.** outrageous   **c.** preserving   **d.** well-meaning

6. Wow! What a great necklace. Those diamonds are _____.
   a. isolated   **b.** magnificent   **c.** fatal   **d.** precise

7. The car race _____ after two of the cars crashed into each other.
   a. came to a standstill   **b.** took root   **c.** made out   **d.** had its work cut out for it

8. It's usually a bad idea to _____ in other people's arguments.
   a. erupt   **b.** transform   **c.** interfere   **d.** commemorate

B. Complete the passage with the correct form of items from the box. One item is extra.

erupt	have its work cut out for it	massive	priceless	tale	preserve	interfere

In the 1800s, a British lieutenant governor in Java, after hearing a (1)_____ of a giant temple in the jungle, began a project to find the lost temple of Borobudur. Eventually the temple was found! Borobudur was a(n) (2)_____ temple—over 35 meters high —that was the center for Buddhist worship around 900 A.D., until it was buried in ash when a nearby volcano (3)_____. After it was rediscovered in the 1800s, people stole (4)_____ works of art from the temple, and weather severely damaged some parts of it. When UNESCO stepped in to repair and (5)_____ the temple, the organization (6)_____. Today, Borobudur is protected as a World Heritage site.

What Do You Think?

1. Would you be interested in visiting the temple of Borobudur? Why or why not? What other World Heritage sites do you know? Which have you visited, or which would you like to visit?

2. Who do you think should spend money to restore old buildings? Should restoration be paid for by local government, the national government, international organizations, or by private companies?

Mr. Right

Before You Read

Answer the following questions.

1. How did your parents meet each other? What are some other common ways for couples to meet?

   _____

   _____

   _____

2. Do you know any couples who met in an interesting way? How did they meet each other?

   _____

   _____

   _____

3. Have you ever watched any "dating shows" on TV? If yes, what do people on the show do?

   _____

   _____

   _____

Target Vocabulary

Match each word with the best meaning.

1. _____ compatible
2. _____ conditional
3. _____ deny
4. _____ exotic
5. _____ gorgeous
6. _____ gossip
7. _____ seal
8. _____ snub
9. _____ sob
10. _____ volunteer

a. to say that something is not true

b. to close something firmly

c. to do work without being paid for it; agree to do something because you want to, not because you were asked to

d. to cry loudly with the body shaking

e. unusual and attractive, especially from a faraway place

f. beautiful; very attractive

g. to talk or write about other people's actions or lives in a negative or untruthful way

h. able to live or work well together

i. to ignore someone in a cold and impolite way

j. depending on; requiring that something be done

When looking for love, people may go to some extreme lengths. They might go on blind dates set up by family and friends. They might write personal ads to place in newspapers. Or they might use a computer to help them in their search for a soul mate by joining an online dating service. Some people have even tried to find their perfect match through game shows on
5 television. Many of these TV dating shows, including *The Bachelor* and *Who Wants to Marry a Multimillionaire?*, have proved to be ratings blockbusters, with millions of viewers watching each week to find out which of the contestants will find true love.

Of all these game shows, perhaps the one with the most unexpected ending was *Mr. Right*, which was shown in England in 2002. On the show, a bachelor, thirty-five-year-old Lance
10 Gerrard-Wright, dated fifteen women to find the one who was his ideal partner. The host of the show was Ulrika Jonsson, an English celebrity originally from Sweden. For seven weeks on the show, Gerrard-Wright took turns going on dates with each of the women, taking them to expensive restaurants and **exotic** locations. He even met the women's families and introduced them to his own. Then at the end of each episode, he would choose between one and three of
15 the contestants with whom he had felt the least **compatible**, and say goodbye to them.

At one point during the series, one contestant **volunteered** to leave because she said she didn't find him attractive. After two dates she said she had had enough, and she couldn't see it working, "He wasn't my cup of tea." In another episode the woman he was on a date with burst into tears when he called her by another contestant's name. "You called me by another
20 girl's name. I can't believe you did that. I really liked you," she **sobbed**.

But in the final episode, the woman he eventually chose decided she didn't want to marry him after all. "I think you've chosen me because you have to choose someone," she said. Maybe this was because she already knew he had fallen in love—with the show's host!

After leaving the show, Gerrard-Wright and Jonsson were seen dining together and attending
25 parties around London more and more often. Finally, on May 1, 2003, Gerrard-Wright proposed to Jonsson on the steps of St. Paul's Cathedral.[1] And she accepted his proposal right away, although it was a **conditional** acceptance. Jonsson has two children from previous relationships—an eight-year-old son, Cameron, and a two-year-old daughter, Bo. She had to make sure that they agreed to the marriage. Luckily, they did. Gerrard-Wright said, "In the end
30 the show did work for me. I grabbed an opportunity to get a girlfriend and I did. Ulrika's **gorgeous**."

The happy couple finally tied the knot at Jonsson's home in Sweden on the island of Varmdo. They wanted to keep the ceremony small, so only forty people were invited, including family and friends. There was some **gossip** at the time that Jonsson's friends who did not receive
35 invitations to the wedding felt **snubbed** by her. But the bride and groom did not let that ruin their wedding day.

Has Ulrika Jonsson finally found Mr. Right? Only time will tell. But none of the guests at the wedding could **deny** the happiness in the couple's eyes as the bride and groom left the wedding ceremony with the music of Stevie Wonder[2] playing in the background, "Seen a lot of things in
40 this old world. When I touched them, they did nothing, girl. Ooh baby, here I am, signed, **sealed**, delivered, I'm yours."

_____ **minutes** _____ **seconds** (607 words)

---

[1] **St. Paul's Cathedral** a large church in London, built in the seventeenth century
[2] **Stevie Wonder (1950–)** a famous American singer of soul music

Reading Comprehension

Circle the letter of the best answer.

1. What is this passage mainly about?
   a. how a famous couple met and got married
   b. the best way to meet a husband or wife
   c. why the show *Mr. Right* was a big hit
   d. how to act on a date with a stranger

2. What happened after seven weeks of doing the show?
   a. All of the women won prizes.
   b. Lance asked one of the women to marry him.
   c. One of the women on the show started to cry.
   d. Ulrika asked Lance to marry her.

3. Which of the following did NOT happen during the series?
   a. Lance went on dates with several women.
   b. The candidates went to some very good restaurants.
   c. Lance and Ulrika started dating each other.
   d. The women met Lance's family.

4. Why did some of Ulrika's friends feel upset?
   a. They didn't agree with the marriage.
   b. They weren't asked to come to the wedding.
   c. There weren't enough guests at the wedding.
   d. They didn't like Lance.

5. In Stevie Wonder's song, what is he comparing himself to?
   a. a blind man   **b.** a letter   **c.** a groom   **d.** a baby

Idioms

Find each idiom in the story.

1. **burst into tears (laughter/song)**—*suddenly start crying*
   • Her mother **burst into tears** when the bride said "I do."
   • Sheila is very unpredictable. She often **bursts into tears** for no reason.

2. **go to (any/great) lengths**—*do something extreme to succeed*
   • He said he would **go to any lengths** to get the job.
   • She **went to great lengths** to get front row seats at the concert.

3. **be not (one's) cup of tea**—*not be something that one likes*
   • Golf is **not really my cup of tea**. I prefer basketball.
   • Although he was a great artist, teaching art was **not his cup of tea**.

Vocabulary Reinforcement

A. Circle the letter of the word or phrase that best completes the sentence.

1. That movie is about a man who is falsely _____ of a crime he didn't commit.
   a. denied   **b.** snubbed   **c.** accused   **d.** sacrificed

2. I don't think I'll join you on Saturday night. Karaoke is just _____.
   a. not my cup of tea   **b.** gone to lengths   **c.** magnificent   **d.** gorgeous

3. If we don't send the Klevbergs an invitation to the party, they might feel _____.
   a. settled   **b.** sealed   **c.** sobbed   **d.** snubbed

4. People told me he and his wife were having problems, but that was just _____.
   a. acceptance   **b.** gossip   **c.** exotic   **d.** conditional

5. She _____ the envelope and put a stamp on it.
   a. denied   **b.** sealed   **c.** snubbed   **d.** sobbed

6. This expensive restaurant serves a lot of _____ drinks that I've never heard of.
   a. compatible   **b.** conservative   **c.** exotic   **d.** isolated

7. The frightened child _____ on her father's shoulder.
   a. sobbed   **b.** commuted   **c.** interfered   **d.** transformed

8. This job offer is _____ on you passing the language test.
   a. conditional   **b.** compatible   **c.** influenced   **d.** adopted

B. Complete the passage with the correct form of items from the box. One item is extra.

burst into tears	conditional	compatible	deny
volunteer	gorgeous	go to great lengths	

Lance Gerrard-Wright (1)_____ to go on the show *Mr. Right* to find his perfect
match. On the show, he had the opportunity to date many (2)_____ women in
order to find the one he was most (3)_____ with. Although he (4)_____
to wine and dine the women, not all of his dates worked out. In fact, one of his dates
(5)_____ when he called her by the wrong name. But in the end, no one can
(6)_____ that things worked out well for Mr. Gerrard-Wright. He finally married
Ulrika Jonsson, the host of the show.

What Do You Think?

1. Do you think Ulrika and Lance will be happy together? What makes you think so?

2. What are some other celebrity marriages that you know? Why do you think that celebrity
   marriages often don't last?

Gift-Giving Etiquette

Before You Read

Answer the following questions.

1. Who do you usually give gifts to? What kinds of gifts do you give them?

   _____

2. Is it usual to give gifts to business partners in your country? What would be a suitable gift?

   _____

3. Are there any special customs or rules about gift-giving in your country?

   _____

Target Vocabulary

Match each word with the best meaning.

1. _____ (in)appropriate	**a.** general way of doing something
2. _____ aspect	**b.** (not) correct or suitable
3. _____ contrast	**c.** a difference or comparison between two things
4. _____ customary	**d.** quiet; not light; not loud
5. _____ etiquette	**e.** a feature; a part of something
6. _____ flashy	**f.** usually done in a particular situation
7. _____ frustrating	**g.** expected and correct way of behaving
8. _____ process	**h.** noticeable, but in a bad way; showing off
9. _____ subdued	**i.** with poor taste or poor artistic quality; not suitable for a polite situation
10. _____ vulgar	
	j. causing a feeling of anger by preventing someone from doing something they want to do

In the early part of the twentieth century, an American woman named Emily Post wrote a book on **etiquette**. This book explained the proper behavior Americans should follow in many different social situations, from birthday parties to funerals. This book, *The Emily Post Book of Etiquette*, continues to sell well today, although some of the rules Ms. Post gave have been
5   updated by the publishers over the years. But in modern society, it is not enough to simply know the proper rules for behavior in your own country. International travel for work and pleasure now makes it necessary for people to understand the rules of etiquette in other cultures as well.

Take, for example, the etiquette required in giving and receiving gifts. As a business traveler, it
10   might be necessary from time to time to give a gift to a client or coworker from another culture. Or, as a visitor in another country, a person might receive a gift of welcome or of thanks from members of the host culture. In both giving and receiving gifts, one should not assume that the rules of etiquette are the same or even similar to the rules in one's own culture.

Cultural differences may appear even in such simple **processes** as giving or receiving a gift. In
15   Western cultures, a gift can be handed over to the receiver with relatively little ceremony. When a gift is offered, the receiver typically takes the gift while expressing her or his thanks. However, in some Asian cultures, the act of giving is an important **aspect** of gift-giving, and this process may appear confusing or **frustrating** to Westerners. In Chinese culture, a receiver will typically refuse to accept the gift at first, with the understanding between the giver and
20   receiver that after being turned down several times, the gift will be accepted. In addition, to show respect for the receiver, it is **customary** in several Asian cultures to use two hands when offering a gift to another person.

After receiving a gift, tradition may demand that the person open the gift right away or, alternatively, wait before opening the gift. In many Western cultures, etiquette requires the
25   receiver to open the gift immediately and show appreciation for the thoughtfulness of the giver. In Asian cultures, on the other hand, the gift may be accepted with appreciation and then set aside to be opened later. The gift will then be opened in private to avoid appearing greedy or impatient.

Another tip for cross-cultural gift-giving relates to wrapping presents, especially in choosing
30   the color of paper used to wrap a gift. In Japan, for example, white or very bright colors are traditionally not good choices for wrapping a gift. In Japanese culture, white is the color associated with mourning and bright colors may be considered by some people to be **vulgar** because they are too **flashy**. Plain white and black are also to be avoided when wrapping presents in China, because of the relation of these colors to funerals. Joyful colors such as red,
35   yellow, and pink are preferred in Chinese culture. In **contrast**, Europeans seem to prefer more **subdued** colors for wrapping presents. A good rule of thumb for wrapping gifts, especially for business travelers, is to travel with unwrapped gifts, and then wrap the gift with paper bought in the country where the gift will be given.

Finally, when choosing the **appropriate** gift to give, a good rule to bear in mind is the
40   following: "Never give vodka to Russians, chocolate to Belgians, or beer to Germans." It is better to travel with quality gifts from one's own region or culture. These are much more likely to be appreciated in other cultures because of their unique nature.

 _____ **minutes** _____ **seconds** (620 words)

Reading Comprehension

Circle the letter of the best answer.

1. What is the best title for this passage?

   a. The Life of Emily Post

   b. Gift-Giving Seasons around the World

   c. Culturally Appropriate Gift-Giving

   d. The Perfect Business Present

2. Which of the following statements about Ms. Post is true?

   a. She influenced people's behavior.

   b. Few people today know about her.

   c. Her book was mainly aimed at people dealing with other cultures.

   d. All of the above.

3. According to the passage, what should you do when giving a gift to an Asian person?

   a. Wait for the receiver to open it.

   b. Use two hands to hand it over.

   c. Use white wrapping paper.

   d. Apologize and take the gift back if it is turned down at first.

4. According to the article, which of these colors would probably be most suitable for wrapping a present in both China and Japan?

   a. white   **b.** black   **c.** red   **d.** blue

5. According to the passage, what should a business traveler NOT do regarding gifts?

   a. give gifts from his or her own country

   b. give gifts from the country of the host

   c. carry unwrapped gifts

   d. give chocolate, vodka, or beer as gifts

Idioms

Find each idiom in the story.

1. **a rule of thumb**—*an idea of how to do something that can be used most of the time*
   - As a good **rule of thumb** you should spend no more than a quarter of your salary on rent.
   - **A rule of thumb** for good health is to eat five pieces of fruit each day.

2. **bear (something) in mind**—*remember; take into consideration*
   - Don't be too hard on Brian. **Bear in mind** it's his first week at the company.
   - That's a good point; I'll **bear** it **in mind** when I make my decision.

3. **turn (someone/something) down**—*decline or refuse to accept*
   - Jeff was very upset when his girlfriend **turned** his proposal **down**.
   - They offered me the job, but, in the end, I **turned** them **down**.

Vocabulary Reinforcement

A. Circle the letter of the word or phrase that best completes the sentence.

1. In some countries, blowing your nose in public is considered _____.
   a. flashy   **b.** magnificent   **c.** subdued   **d.** vulgar

2. Traveling to different countries is the _____ of my job that I enjoy most.
   a. effect   **b.** aspect   **c.** contrast   **d.** process

3. You seem a bit _____ today. Is something wrong?
   a. flashy   **b.** subdued   **c.** frustrating   **d.** vulgar

4. When you plan the menu for the party on Saturday, _____ some of the guests are vegetarians.
   a. bear in mind   **b.** as a rule   **c.** go to lengths   **d.** pay attention to

5. A lot of people like expensive jewelry, but I find it too _____.
   a. magnificent   **b.** flashy   **c.** subdued   **d.** priceless

6. Buying a house for the first time can be a scary _____.
   a. aspect   **b.** policy   **c.** strategy   **d.** process

7. A diamond engagement ring should, _____, cost two to three months' salary.
   a. frustratingly   **b.** as a rule of thumb   **c.** pricelessly   **d.** as long as

8. Jeans are usually _____ clothing for a formal wedding.
   a. flashy   **b.** subdued   **c.** inappropriate   **d.** customary

B. Complete the passage with the correct form of items from the box. One item is extra.

bear in mind	contrast	customary	etiquette
frustrating	(in)appropriate	turn it down	

When people from different cultures meet, problems may occur because their cultures follow different rules of (1)_____. What may be normal behavior in one culture may seem (2)_____ or even rude in another. Take, for example, the (3)_____ between Western and Asian cultures regarding correct ways of giving and receiving gifts. In some Asian cultures it is (4)_____ to refuse a gift several times before accepting it. Westerners may find it (5)_____ when they offer a gift to someone and the receiver (6)_____.

What Do You Think?

1. Have you ever acted inappropriately when dealing with someone of another culture? Has anyone from another culture ever acted inappropriately with you? If so, what happened?

2. Are there any important cultural rules that a visitor to your country should know? If so, what are they?

Review 6–10

A. Circle the correct answer for each question.

1. Which of these are priceless?	a. old photographs	b. a new car
2. If you have trouble with schoolwork, who should you find?	a. a scholar	b. a tutor
3. Which time is more precise?	a. about 10 A.M.	b. 10:03 A.M.
4. Which of these occurs prior to a wedding?	a. an engagement	b. a honeymoon
5. Who is usually more conservative?	a. young people	b. old people
6. How do people feel when they can't do what they want?	a. snubbed	b. frustrated
7. Which word best describes a red and yellow shirt?	a. flashy	b. subdued
8. Which of these is more likely to glow?	a. a tree	b. a candle
9. Which of these should parents teach their children?	a. ignorance	b. etiquette
10. To most people, missing a party to stay home and take care of a baby is . . .	a. a sacrifice	b. well-meaning

B. Complete the paragraph with the correct form of items from the box. Two items are extra.

commemorate	contrast	customary	exotic	fatal
frustrate	have (one's) work cut out for (one)		isolated	precise
rural	take the day off		transform	

One of the most important annual holidays in the United States each year is Thanksgiving, when it is (1)_____ for Americans to return home to spend time with their whole family. The (2)_____ date of Thanksgiving changes from year to year, but it is always held on the fourth Thursday in November. This Thursday is a public holiday and most people also (3)_____ on Friday to make a four-day weekend.

The history of Thanksgiving goes back to 1621. In 1620, a group of settlers, called pilgrims, left England and sailed across the Atlantic to start a new (4)_____ society in the New World (now called America). They quickly discovered that the new land was a great (5)_____ to England, and they really (6)_____. The winter in the new land was very cold and they arrived too late in the season to grow any food. Because the community was so (7)_____ and far from England, they were unable to get any fresh food. Half of the new settlers died from (8)_____ diseases that winter.

The following spring, the Native Americans saw the pilgrims were having a hard time and decided to help. They showed the pilgrims how to grow corn and other new and (9)_____ plants, and also how to hunt and fish. In 1621, the harvest was very successful, and the pilgrims decided to have a feast to thank the Native Americans for all their help. In following years this feast became an annual event to (10)_____ that first Thanksgiving feast.

C. Circle the odd one out in each group.

1. **a.** precise **b.** exact **c.** specific **d.** general
2. **a.** understanding **b.** knowledge **c.** ignorance **d.** insight
3. **a.** isolated **b.** neighboring **c.** lonely **d.** distant
4. **a.** exotic **b.** uncommon **c.** typical **d.** foreign
5. **a.** gorgeous **b.** magnificent **c.** massive **d.** priceless
6. **a.** gaze **b.** stare **c.** glow **d.** pay attention to
7. **a.** governor **b.** president **c.** prime minister **d.** activist
8. **a.** bring about **b.** cause **c.** put an end to **d.** create
9. **a.** snub **b.** burst into tears **c.** cry **d.** sob
10. **a.** conservative **b.** outrageous **c.** vulgar **d.** flashy

D. Use the clues below to complete the crossword.

Across

1. Waking up early is the _____ of my job that is most difficult.
5. House prices are going through a(n) _____ at the moment, and are very expensive.
8. Please keep away from my desk. I don't want you to _____ with my papers.
10. Even if you don't like someone, you shouldn't _____ them.
11. You shouldn't listen to _____ about other people.
12. This festival is to _____ the end of the war.
16. After you've finished writing your letter, make sure to _____ the envelope.
18. look at something for a long time
19. He was killed in a(n) _____ car accident.
20. I hired a(n) _____ to help me study for the exam.

Down

2. cry loudly
3. The couple realized they weren't _____ and split up.
4. I learned the cheese-making _____ from my grandparents.
6. The prices in this shop are _____. I'm never shopping here again!
7. The _____ number of people killed in the earthquake was unknown, but it was more than ten thousand.
9. I'll drive you to the beach, _____ you help pay for gas.

13. Can you read that sign? I can't _____ what it says from here.
14. a story or legend
15. It is never appropriate to tell _____ jokes in a job interview.
17. Run for your life! The volcano is going to _____!

Interview Techniques

Before You Read

Answer the following questions.

1. Do you know anyone who has been to a job interview recently? If so, who was it and for what job?

   _____

   _____

   _____

2. What should an applicant do to prepare for a job interview?

   _____

   _____

   _____

3. What are some typical questions that are asked in an interview?

   _____

   _____

   _____

Target Vocabulary

Match each word with the best meaning.

1. _____ alert
2. _____ boast
3. _____ candidate
4. _____ colleague
5. _____ ethnic
6. _____ literally
7. _____ perceive
8. _____ pose (a problem)
9. _____ respond
10. _____ structure

a. to answer or reply

b. the way parts are put together or organized (n); to put parts together or organize them (v)

c. someone who is being considered for a position

d. paying full attention to one's surroundings

e. related to one's racial or cultural background

f. present a difficulty

g. to praise oneself (v); something said in praise of oneself (n)

h. according to the exact words

i. become aware of something through the senses or by thinking

j. a person with whom one works

Everyone is nervous when they go to an interview for a new job. But, being well-prepared for the interview can really reduce your stress level when you walk in the door to the interview room. One way to prepare for an interview is to think about the typical questions interviewers ask. If you know which questions are likely to come up in the interview, you can prepare your answers
5   beforehand. Then, when you are talking with the interviewer, you will make a much better impression.

Probably the most frequently asked question in any job interview is not really a question at all. It is the request, "Tell me about yourself." The interviewer's purpose in asking this question is to elicit[1] information related to work and related to the job opening. Some people make the mistake
10   of taking this request **literally**, and answering by giving their life history. In fact, the best points to focus on when answering this question are past work experience, education, and extracurricular activities.[2] Of these three, in most cases work experience carries a lot more weight than where you went to school or the clubs you were involved in.

Another very common question that comes up in interviews is "Why do you want to work for
15   this company?" A surefire[3] way to get your name crossed off the **candidate** list for a job is by not having an answer to this question. If you don't have an answer ready for this question, you are letting the interviewer know that you haven't done much research about the company or the job you are interviewing for. Candidates who can give detailed answers about the **perceived** benefits of working for a particular company make a much better impression on interviewers. Some good
20   things to brush up on before an interview are the company's philosophy, goals, products, organizational **structure**, and so forth.

Two other questions that many people find difficult in interviews are "What are your strengths?" and "What is your biggest weakness?" People have a hard time answering the first question because it feels like **boasting** in some ways. But an interview is no time to be shy or modest! The
25   second question **poses** a problem because the answer needs to be a weakness that sounds like a strength. For example, you could answer that sometimes you work too hard, especially trying to make up work that a **colleague** is having trouble with or has not done. A good tip to keep in mind is to mention how you are trying to improve this weakness. For example, you could say that when you realize you are doing the work of others, you stop and ask yourself if there is a
30   better way to help out your coworker.

Along with considering these common interview questions, it is also helpful to bear in mind the types of questions that should not be asked during an interview. In many Western countries, in particular, there are laws that restrict the kinds of questions that employers can ask. For instance, questions related to **ethnicity**, family, health, or religion are generally off limits in an interview.
35   Sometimes interviewers may slip up and ask questions along these lines before the official interview begins as a way to break the ice. In such cases, you can decide how to **respond**. If you don't feel comfortable giving the interviewer such personal information, simply don't.

A final suggestion for preparing for an interview is to go into the interview with your own questions to ask. By asking the interviewer questions about the company or about the position,
40   you are showing interest and enthusiasm for the job. Stay **alert** during the interview for opportunities to naturally bring up one of the questions you have prepared. Usually it is a good idea to write down five questions you would like to ask, but don't be surprised if you can't ask all or any of them in the interview.

 _____ **minutes** _____ **seconds** (657 words)

---

[1] **elicit** to get; to bring out
[2] **extracurricular activities** activities done outside school or work. The prefix "extra-" means "outside."
[3] **surefire** certain to work as expected

Reading Comprehension

Circle the letter of the best answer.

1. What is the passage mainly about?
   - **a.** actions to avoid during an interview
   - **b.** body language that interviewers watch for
   - **c.** embarrassing interview experiences
   - **d.** typical interview questions and responses

2. When asked to tell about yourself, what should be your main focus?
   - **a.** your family
   - **b.** your past jobs
   - **c.** your hobbies
   - **d.** kinds of work you enjoy

3. Which is NOT something that is important to know before an interview?
   - **a.** how the company plans to grow or change
   - **b.** the company's philosophy
   - **c.** the background of the interviewer
   - **d.** the different departments of the company and how they relate to each other

4. According to the passage, which type of question is inappropriate for an interviewer to ask?
   - **a.** How many children do you have?
   - **b.** What is one of your weak points?
   - **c.** Where did you last work?
   - **d.** Why do you want to work for this company?

5. Why should you prepare your own questions before the interview?
   - **a.** to let the interviewer know your strong points
   - **b.** to help the interviewer feel relaxed
   - **c.** to make the interview last longer
   - **d.** to seem enthusiastic

Idioms

Find each idiom in the story.

1. **carry weight**—*to have importance*
   - The last piece of evidence did not **carry** much **weight** during the trial.
   - The fact that he has a degree from Harvard **carries** a lot of **weight** in my opinion.

2. **brush up on**—*practice to relearn or improve an old skill*
   - Before I took the exam, I had to **brush up on** the math I learned in high school.
   - She's taking a class to **brush up on** her French before she moves to Paris.

3. **break the ice**—*do something to create a more relaxed atmosphere*
   - On the first day of class, the teacher planned a game to help **break the ice**.
   - She made a few jokes to **break the ice** at the start of their date.

Vocabulary Reinforcement

A. Circle the letter of the word or phrase that best completes the sentence.

1. He was sleepy, so he drank some coffee to keep himself awake and _____.
   a. alert   b. customary   c. ethnic   d. appropriate

2. I like to try _____ foods from other cultures.
   a. candidate   b. vulgar   c. ethnic   d. structured

3. Many teachers _____ their lessons into five or ten minute blocks of time.
   a. pose   b. process   c. respond   d. structure

4. No one appreciated the way she _____ about her father's wealth.
   a. alerted   b. boasted   c. contrasted   d. posed

5. Several of my _____ told me about the presentation you gave.
   a. activities   b. colleagues   c. impressions   d. candidates

6. The party was very _____. Everyone just sat and talked quietly all night.
   a. alert   b. ethnic   c. literal   d. subdued

7. We served drinks and snacks at our club meetings to help _____ for new members.
   a. break the ice b. brush up   c. carry weight   d. turn down

8. What do you _____ is the author's point in this story?
   a. boast   b. perceive   c. respond   d. structure

B. Complete the passage with the correct form of items from the box. One item is extra.

brush up on	candidates	literally	pose a problem
respond	alert	carry more weight	

When there is a job opening in a company, (1)_____ usually have to go through
an interview. How people (2)_____ to questions in these interviews determines
who will be chosen for the job. Therefore, it's a good idea to (3)_____ common
questions and good answers before going into an interview. When told, "Tell me about
yourself," someone who (4)_____ gives his or her life story, by and large, won't
be hired. Information related to work experience (5)_____ in answering this
question than information about family and hobbies. Also, questions asking about strengths
and weaknesses may (6)_____ for many people if they have not prepared answers
prior to the interview.

What Do You Think?

1. Apart from responding well to questions, what else can make a good impression during
   an interview?

2. What kind of job would you like to have? How can you get experience in this field
   before you actually get a job?

The Love Bug

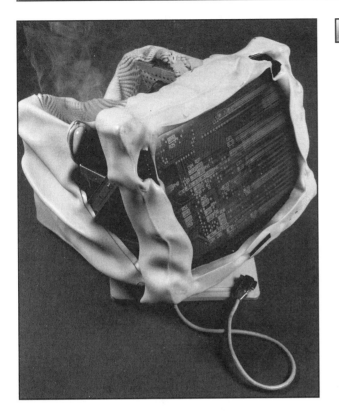

Before You Read

Answer the following questions.

1. What do you know about computer viruses?

   _____

   _____

   _____

2. Have you, or has anyone you know, ever been affected by a computer virus? What happened?

   _____

   _____

   _____

3. What kind of person do you think creates a computer virus?

   _____

   _____

   _____

Target Vocabulary

Match each word with the best meaning.

1. _____ attach
2. _____ chaos
3. _____ culprit
4. _____ devastating
5. _____ emerge
6. _____ infect
7. _____ innocent
8. _____ malicious
9. _____ unleash
10. _____ unsuspecting

a. to appear; to come from a place where something or someone could not be seen

b. join something to something else

c. a completely disorganized and confused state

d. give someone a disease or sickness

e. not guilty; harmless; pure

f. unprepared for trouble; trusting

g. release a powerful force

h. a person who is guilty of doing something wrong

i. wanting to hurt people or cause damage

j. completely destroying

On May 4, 2000, the **devastating** "Love Bug" computer virus was **unleashed** on the Internet. The virus originated in the Philippines, but it quickly spread westward around the globe as individuals and businesses began their mornings by opening their e-mails.

The Love Bug traveled via e-mail attachment. A person would receive an e-mail with the subject
5   line "I LOVE YOU." Naturally, the receiver would be curious to see who had sent them such a nice message. Upon opening the e-mail, the receiver would read the lines, "kindly check the **attached** LOVELETTER coming from me." The **unsuspecting** individual would then click on the e-mail's attachment and unleash computer **chaos**. While the computer user would sit and wonder why they couldn't see a love letter on the screen, the attachment was busy within the
10   computer. The program would search the user's e-mail address book and send copies of the "I LOVE YOU" e-mail to everyone listed, and then the **malicious** program went on to delete various music, video, and image files within the computer.

As the Love Bug traveled around the world, it **infected** businesses and government computers all across Europe and North America. Japan missed out on much of the damage caused by the virus
15   because the country was on a public holiday most of that week. China also escaped any major problems caused by the virus. But in Europe, 80 percent of the e-mail companies in Sweden had to shut down because their systems were overloaded by the virus. Businesses in Switzerland, Denmark, and Norway were also heavily hit by the Love Bug. And in England, the troublesome e-mail message caused problems for British Telecom, the BBC, and even the British House of
20   Commons.[1]

Then the Love Bug jumped across the Atlantic to invade the United States. Businesses in the United States did a little better than those in Europe simply because they had been warned about the spreading virus beforehand. But even that forewarning did not stop the Love Bug from temporarily shutting down e-mail services in Ford Motor Company, the ABC television network,
25   and the United Nations offices. It even turned up in the computers of some senators in Washington D.C. and in high security government computers.

Internet security companies quickly went to work to create anti-virus programs that would protect computers from the Love Bug. But another problem quickly **emerged**. Just as the first wave of the virus was passing, other variations of the Love Bug began to appear. These
30   variations appeared as **innocent** Mother's Day messages and even as Love Bug anti-virus downloads. Obviously, hackers who were infected by the original virus used the destructive program they were sent to create their own virus e-mails. By the time it was finished, the Love Bug cost businesses and computer users around the world more than $10 billion.

And who was finally to blame for all this damage? The suspected **culprit** turned out to be a
35   twenty-four-year-old computer science student in Manila named Onel de Guzman. Of course, he never admitted to sending the Love Bug. He only said he helped create the original program using ideas from the thesis[2] he planned to write for his degree. But his professors rejected the thesis idea, and de Guzman dropped out of college.

Surprisingly, de Guzman did not go to jail for what he did. When the Love Bug was released in
40   May, the Philippines did not have any laws against high-tech crimes such as this. The country quickly passed a law the next month, but the new law could not be used to punish de Guzman for his past crime. So in the end, no one ended up being punished for creating the virus.

_____ **minutes** _____ **seconds** (615 words)

---

[1] **British Telecom** a British telecommunications company; **the BBC** the British Broadcasting Corporation (television and radio); **House of Commons** section of the British government with representatives elected by the population
[2] **thesis** a study made and written by a student as part of a university degree

Reading Comprehension

Circle the letter of the best answer.

1. What is the main idea of this reading?
   a. a computer virus that turned out to be a hoax
   b. a destructive computer virus in the past
   c. the first computer virus in history
   d. ways to protect your computer from viruses

2. Where did the Love Bug start?
   a. Asia   b. Australia   c. Europe   d. North America

3. Why didn't the Love Bug do much damage in Japan?
   a. Japan heard about the virus spreading in America.
   b. Japanese businesses were closed at the time.
   c. Japanese computers couldn't open the e-mail.
   d. Japanese programmers used an anti-virus program.

4. Which is true about the second wave of Love Bug viruses?
   a. Anti-virus programs could not stop them.
   b. Other hackers changed the original virus.
   c. People returned them to senders of the infected messages.
   d. The programmer of the original virus wrote them.

5. Why wasn't de Guzman sent to prison?
   a. He moved to the Philippines before police caught him.
   b. His computer was infected with the virus.
   c. The court found him innocent.
   d. There was no law against what he did.

Idioms

Find each idiom in the story.

1. **drop out (of something)**—*quit*
   - He **dropped out of** school and got a job delivering pizzas.
   - The other candidate may **drop out of** the race to become governor.

2. **miss out on**—*not get; not participate in something that would have been good*
   - If you don't reply today, you might **miss out on** this great opportunity.
   - She **missed out on** the party because she was busy studying.

3. **turn up**—*appear*
   - The book I thought I had lost **turned up** at my friend's house.
   - Don't worry about your dog. She'll **turn up** when she gets hungry.

Vocabulary Reinforcement

A. Circle the letter of the word or phrase that best completes the sentence.

1. A(n) _____ earthquake caused a lot of damage to the city.
   a. devastating   **b.** innocent   **c.** malicious   **d.** unsuspecting

2. Let's get there early so we don't _____ any part of the presentation.
   a. brush up on   **b.** drop out of   **c.** break the ice with   **d.** miss out on

3. Please _____ your store receipt to the letter before you mail it.
   a. infect   **b.** attach   **c.** spread   **d.** alert

4. The female candidate finally _____ as the winner in the election.
   a. emerged   **b.** overloaded   **c.** responded   **d.** unleashed

5. The police finally caught the _____ at the airport.
   a. aspect   **b.** chaos   **c.** culprit   **d.** etiquette

6. There was _____ in the classroom. The students were shouting and throwing things at each other.
   a. boasting   **b.** chaos   **c.** a culprit   **d.** forewarning

7. Although this game can be very _____ at first, don't give up.
   a. devastating   **b.** frustrating   **c.** innocent   **d.** malicious

8. You found your purse! Where did it _____?
   a. bear in mind   **b.** drop out   **c.** miss out   **d.** turn up

B. Complete the passage with the correct form of items from the box. One item is extra.

turn up   infect   malicious   drop out of   innocent   unleash   unsuspecting

In the year 2000, one of the worst computer viruses in history was (1)_____ on the Internet. This virus was called the "Love Bug," and it (2)_____ computers around the world. The virus appeared as a(n) (3)_____ love letter sent via e-mail. However, attached to this letter was a(n) (4)_____ program that copied itself and went out to other people. Then the program went on to delete files from the (5)_____ victim's computer. The person finally blamed for creating the virus was a college student in the Philippines who had (6)_____ college.

What Do You Think?

1. Do you think that the authorities did the right thing by not punishing de Guzman just because there was no law covering what he had done? If not, what should they have done?

2. Do you think that overall computers have had a positive or negative impact on people's lives? What are some of the pros and cons of computers in modern society?

Crime and Punishment 13

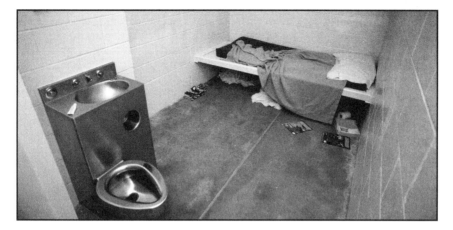

Before You Read

Answer the following questions.

1. Do you think that the laws in your country are strict? Why do (or don't) you think so? Are there any laws you don't agree with?

   _____

2. How are criminals usually punished in your country?

   _____

3. Which country do you think has the largest number of prisoners?

   _____

Target Vocabulary

Match each word with the best meaning.

1. _____ convict
2. _____ deter
3. _____ enforce
4. _____ law-abiding
5. _____ offend
6. _____ penalty
7. _____ retain
8. _____ revenge
9. _____ sensational
10. _____ supposedly

a. as it seems; as it is assumed

b. a prisoner sentenced to jail for a crime (n); to find someone guilty in a court (v)

c. a punishment given for breaking rules or laws

d. keep possession of something

e. put someone off something; stop or prevent someone from doing something

f. to make people obey rules or laws

g. commit a crime; to displease or annoy

h. doing something to hurt someone as repayment for something

i. well-behaved; obeying the law

j. very exciting or interesting; exciting in a negative way

Almost everyone accepts the fact that crime can never be wiped out entirely. Thus, control of crime becomes the focus of police and governments around the world. The question lawmakers must answer is, "Which system of criminal punishment works best for society?" Each country has developed its own ideas for solutions to this question, and these solutions then determine how
5   criminals are punished under different systems. However, there are four main ideas behind the punishment of criminals, none of which has proven 100 percent effective. These are *deterrence*, *retribution*, *rehabilitation*, and *incapacitation*.

The aim of deterrence is to prevent people from committing crimes by making the **penalties** more severe than any benefit that might come from committing a crime. This theory aims to **deter** criminals
10   from repeating a crime in the future. These systems also try to deter others in society by using the criminal as an example of what can happen to a person if he or she is caught committing crimes.

Some systems look only to get retribution, or **revenge**, against criminals. Retributive theories of punishment are behind the ancient expression, "an eye for an eye, a tooth for a tooth." This idea of getting even is the oldest form of justice. It says that a criminal who causes a victim to suffer
15   should be made to suffer him- or herself.

Rehabilitation is another philosophy by which many systems of punishment operate. The goal of these systems is to return a former criminal to society after a required period of treatment and training, usually in prison. The idea is to try to help change the person's behavior and attitude so that he or she becomes a **law-abiding** citizen. A major problem with the current system of
20   rehabilitation in the United States is that most criminals return to crime after they have **supposedly** been rehabilitated. Two-thirds of those released from prison each year are re-arrested within three years. As a result, many people feel that rehabilitation of criminals just doesn't work.

A goal of criminal punishments involving imprisonment is incapacitation. This refers to the removing of the criminal from society by placing them in prison, where they are physically
25   incapable of **reoffending**. This type of punishment is displayed in the "three strikes and you're out" laws of California, where a criminal who has repeatedly committed crimes, and has been **convicted** of serious crimes three times, is imprisoned for the rest of his or her life.

Imprisonment as a form of punishment is used in all countries of the world. In 2003, there were an estimated 8.75 million prisoners around the world. The country with the largest prison population,
30   by far, is the United States, with around two million people behind bars.

The most extreme form of punishment is capital punishment, in which the criminal is executed, or put to death. Today, capital punishment is still used in eighty-three countries, usually for severe crimes such as murder, rape, kidnapping, and treason.[1] Another seventy-six countries have done away with it completely. In others, capital punishment remains only officially in law books but is
35   rarely used—fifteen countries have capital punishment, but only **enforce** it during war time, while twenty-one countries, despite officially **retaining** the death penalty, never enforce it.

Many people feel that society is becoming more dangerous, and that rates of crime are increasing. In a recent survey in the United Kingdom, almost two-thirds of respondents felt that crime had increased in the previous two years. However, actual crime figures revealed that crime had
40   decreased nine percent on the previous year, and was actually at its lowest rate in two decades. Why is there such a discrepancy[2] between perceived crime rates and actual crime rates? Many people point the finger at the media. They think that the media's heavy focus on crimes, particularly violent or **sensational** ones, has led people to believe that crime rates are rocketing.[3]

_____ **minutes** _____ **seconds** (647 words)

---

[1] **rape** forcing someone to have sex against their will; **kidnapping** taking a person and asking for money to return them; **treason** going against your country, e.g., by helping the enemies of the country
[2] **discrepancy** a difference between what something should be and what it actually is
[3] **rocketing** increasing very rapidly

Reading Comprehension

Circle the letter of the best answer.

1. What is NOT discussed in this passage?
   a. theories behind the punishment of criminals
   b. different ways of punishing criminals
   c. arguments against capital punishment
   d. ways in which punishments vary in different countries

2. The fact that many criminals reoffend is a major argument against . . .
   a. deterrence. b. retribution. c. rehabilitation. d. incapacitation.

3. In some ancient societies, a man who accidentally killed another man's child would have his own child put to death. This is an example of . . .
   a. deterrence. b. retribution. c. rehabilitation. d. incapacitation.

4. How many countries around the world have the death penalty, at least in theory?
   a. 76 b. 83 c. 98 d. 119

5. What did the survey performed in the United Kingdom reveal?
   a. Crime rates have been increasing over the last two years.
   b. The media tend not to report violent crime.
   c. Most people's impression of crime rates is mistaken.
   d. Britain is safer now than at any time in the past.

Idioms

Find each idiom in the story.

1. **get even (with someone)**—*have revenge on someone; pay someone back for something bad he or she has done*
   • Mike wanted to **get even with** Larry because Larry had called him a liar.
   • Try to forget what she said. You shouldn't waste time trying to **get even with** her.

2. **do away with**—*get rid of something; remove something completely (often officially)*
   • When did the professor **do away with** checking class attendance?
   • Tom has **done away with** all of his credit cards. He has cut them all into pieces.

3. **point the finger at**—*accuse someone of something; blame someone for something*
   • You should take the blame for your own mistakes rather than **pointing the finger at** others.
   • When the company was forced to close, many people **pointed the finger at** the new manager.

Vocabulary Reinforcement

A. Circle the letter of the word or phrase that best completes the sentence.

1. I've never met the new teacher, but _____ she's very good.
   a. unsuspectingly   **b.** initially   **c.** sensationally   **d.** supposedly

2. After she got married, Hillary, rather than taking her husband's name, _____ her own.
   a. retained   **b.** enforced   **c.** attached   **d.** perceived

3. In many countries there are laws that still exist, but are never _____.
   a. retained   **b.** enforced   **c.** attached   **d.** perceived

4. The ex-prisoner had only been out of prison for three days before he _____ again.
   a. revenged   **b.** boasted   **c.** offended   **d.** alerted

5. Although most places have _____ working on Saturday, some countries still require workers to go to the office on the weekend.
   a. got even with   **b.** done away with   **c.** pointed the finger at   **d.** dropped out of

6. No one knew for sure who had stolen the money, but many people _____ Guy.
   a. pointed the finger at   **b.** convicted   **c.** unleashed   **d.** got even with

7. The criminal thought he had gotten away with the murder, but he ended up being _____.
   a. offended   **b.** convicted   **c.** unleashed   **d.** subdued

8. That's a terrible story. You shouldn't spread such _____ gossip.
   a. law-abiding   **b.** malicious   **c.** unsuspecting   **d.** innocent

B. Complete the passage with the correct form of items from the box. One item is extra.

convict	deter	law-abiding	penalty	retain	revenge	sensational

There are various philosophies that guide different societies in determining (1)_____ for criminals. Some societies use harsh punishments to (2)_____ other people from committing the same crime. Other philosophies of punishment look for rehabilitation, while others look for (3)_____—they just want to get even with the offenders. No matter which philosophy a society adopts, all nations around the world have established prisons to hold criminals after they have been (4)_____, and keep them away from other, (5)_____ members of society. Interestingly, a United Kingdom survey has revealed a widespread, but mistaken, belief that crime is increasing in British society. Perhaps this point of view is due to the way the media tends to focus on (6)_____ crime.

What Do You Think?

1. What do you think should be the main aim of punishment: deterrence, retribution, rehabilitation, or incapacitation? Why? What do you think are the pros and cons of each?

2. Does your country use the death penalty? Are you in favor of it? Why or why not? If yes, what kinds of crimes should it be used for? If not, how should very serious crimes be punished?

The Tango

Before You Read

Answer the following questions.

1. Is dancing popular in your country? If yes, what kinds of dance are popular?

   _____

   _____

   _____

2. How do you think that new forms of dance begin?

   _____

   _____

   _____

3. What do you know about the tango?

   _____

   _____

   _____

Target Vocabulary

Match each word with the best meaning.

1. _____ academy
2. _____ ambassador
3. _____ approve (of)
4. _____ embassy
5. _____ evident
6. _____ fluid
7. _____ immigrant
8. _____ initially
9. _____ intense
10. _____ seek

a. to look for something

b. to allow or permit; to admire or agree with

c. the highest level government official who represents a country in a foreign capital city

d. at first

e. a person who moves to another country to live

f. the offices of a country's official staff in a foreign country

g. strong (for a feeling or emotion)

h. a private school or college

i. plain; clear; easy to see

j. smooth, graceful (adj); a liquid (n)

Argentina in the late nineteenth century was an exciting place. Around 1870, it was experiencing an economic boom, and the capital, Buenos Aires, attracted many people. Farmers and ranchers, called *gauchos* in Argentina, came to the city to find jobs in the slaughterhouses[1] and the meatpacking industry. A flood of **immigrants** from Spain and Italy also came to Buenos Aires
5   **seeking** jobs. These jobs did not pay well, and the gauchos felt lonely and frustrated with their new life in the city. As the unhappy gauchos and new immigrants mixed together in the poor parts of the city, the dance known as the tango evolved.

Initially, the tango was a dance of the lower classes. It was danced in the bars and streets of Buenos Aires. At that time there were many fewer women than men, so if a man didn't want to be
10   left out and wanted to practice the new dance, his only choice was to dance with another man. Groups of men would get together to practice so that they could attract the attention of the few available women. Gradually, the dance spread into the upper classes of Argentinean society and became more respectable.

In Europe at this time, **intense** interest in dance from around the world was beginning. This
15   interest in international dance was especially **evident** in Paris. Every kind of dance from ballet to belly dancing[2] could be found on the stages of the Paris theaters. Tango dancers from Argentina arrived in Europe on board the boats carrying beef from Argentina. They began to draw the interest of the public as they performed their passionate dance in the cabarets[3] and cafés. Not everyone **approved** of the new dance, however. In fact, it raised a few eyebrows among the more
20   conservative members of society, who found the tango a little too shocking. However, the dance did find enough supporters so that even the tango's many critics could not put an end to the spreading popularity of the dance.

In the early 1900s, dance masters in both Paris and London developed more modest versions of the tango to teach to their students. These students then carried the tango into the ballrooms of
25   Europe. Two forms of the tango emerged at this time—the **fluid**, stylish Paris tango and the stiffer, more conservative British tango. Neither of these tamed tangos carried the raw passion of the original Argentine tango.

Soldiers who returned to the United States from World War I brought the tango to North America. However, Rudolf Valentino, who danced the tango in the 1921 film *The Four Horsemen*
30   *of the Apocalypse*, was really responsible for spreading the tango across America. The tango danced in the ballrooms of the United States closely resembled the stiff, proper British tango.

The tango reached Japan in 1926, thanks mainly to one man—Baron Tsunayoshi "Tsunami" Megata. This Japanese nobleman had been living in Europe for six years when he returned to Tokyo in 1926. When he returned to Japan, he took with him a handful of tango records and an
35   excellent understanding of the Paris tango. Baron Megata wasted no time in setting up a dance **academy** in Tokyo in which he could teach his wealthy friends the tango and other popular ballroom dances of Europe. Around 1930, British dance masters began setting up their own dance schools in Kobe, and the British tango soon became the most popular version of the tango danced in Japan. Baron Megata is reported to have said, "Whenever you dance, remember you should feel
40   as though you are in love with your partner, even if you have just met (him)."

The popularity of tango continues to grow in many parts of the world, including Asia. In Japan, the 1996 film *Shall We Dance?*, which featured flamenco and tango dancing, led to a dance boom around the country, and in 2003, the Argentinean **embassy** in Seoul hired a local tango dancer to act as a kind of dance **ambassador**, and promote tango dancing throughout South Korea.

   _____ **minutes** _____ **seconds** (671 words)

---

[1] **slaughterhouse** a place where animals are killed for food
[2] **belly dancing** a Middle Eastern style of dancing where a female dancer moves her hips and stomach quickly
[3] **cabaret** a type of nightclub where the audience eat and drink during the performance

Reading Comprehension

Circle the letter of the best answer.

1. What is the best title for this passage?
   - **a.** The History of the Tango
   - **b.** How to Dance the Tango
   - **c.** The Modern Tango Boom
   - **d.** The Tango in Argentina

2. Which statement about the early days of tango is true?
   - **a.** It was usually danced by wealthier members of society.
   - **b.** It was first danced on rural farms and ranches.
   - **c.** It was created in Spain and Italy and brought to Argentina.
   - **d.** It was often danced by two members of the same sex.

3. Where did the people of Paris first see the dance?
   - **a.** on boats
   - **b.** in theaters
   - **c.** in cafés
   - **d.** in ballrooms

4. According to the passage, the most passionate form of tango was danced in which country?
   - **a.** France
   - **b.** England
   - **c.** Argentina
   - **d.** Japan

5. Which statement about Baron Tsunayoshi is NOT true?
   - **a.** He introduced the tango to Japan after living in Europe.
   - **b.** He was most familiar with the form of tango danced in France.
   - **c.** He taught other styles of dance in addition to tango.
   - **d.** He taught the tango at dance schools in Kobe.

Idioms

Find each idiom in the story.

1. **raise eyebrows**—*cause someone to feel surprised or disapproving*
   - The artist's new work should **raise** a few **eyebrows** at the gallery.
   - Harry **raised** a few **eyebrows** at work by going for an interview with another company.

2. **be left out**—*not be included in something*
   - Joanna's little sister was always **left out** when the older children played soccer.
   - Can you please check this invitation list carefully? I don't want to **leave** anyone **out** by mistake.

3. **thanks to**—*because of*
   - I managed to pass the exams, **thanks to** my tutor's help.
   - **Thanks to** Ray coming late, we missed the train.

Vocabulary Reinforcement

A. Circle the letter of the word or phrase that best completes the sentence.

1. Both countries said they were _____ a peaceful solution to the problem.
   a. enforcing   **b.** brushing up on   **c.** seeking   **d.** contrasting

2. She _____ when she married a man who was thirty years younger than her.
   a. pointed the finger   **b.** raised a few eyebrows   **c.** went to lengths   **d.** carried weight

3. I really don't _____ of smoking in restaurants.
   a. approve   **b.** my cup of tea   **c.** offend   **d.** sob

4. I need to go to the Turkish _____ to get a visa before my vacation.
   a. embassy   **b.** ambassador   **c.** academy   **d.** immigrant

5. I have the most _____ pain in the back of my leg. I must have injured it.
   a. intense   **b.** initial   **c.** evident   **d.** fluid

6. The French _____ to Moscow was famous for her magnificent parties.
   a. culprit   **b.** embassy   **c.** immigrant   **d.** ambassador

7. Although she knows a lot about the subject, this just wasn't _____ in the essay she gave to the teacher.
   a. intense   **b.** evident   **c.** retained   **d.** supposed

8. Graham didn't know anyone at the party, so he felt quite _____.
   a. malicious   **b.** unsuspecting   **c.** turned down   **d.** left out

B. Complete the passage with the correct form of items from the box. One item is extra.

academy	evident	fluid	immigrant	initially	raise eyebrows	thanks to

The tango evolved in Argentina in the late 1800s, (1)_____ among poor
(2)_____ and farmers living in Buenos Aires. Eventually the tango made it to
Europe, and the intense passion of the dance excited many people. Although it
(3)_____among conservative audiences, dance masters in both France and England
began to teach modified versions of the tango. In French dance (4)_____, students
learned a style of the tango that was smooth and (5)_____, while the British schools
taught a stiffer style. After soldiers from World War I took the tango back to North America,
the dance then spread to Japan, (6)_____ Baron Tsunayoshi Megata.

What Do You Think?

1. Does your country have any traditional dances? If so, what are they? Do you know how to dance them?

2. Does your country have an immigrant population? If yes, where are they from? What have those immigrants brought to your country?

Cloning Extinct Animals

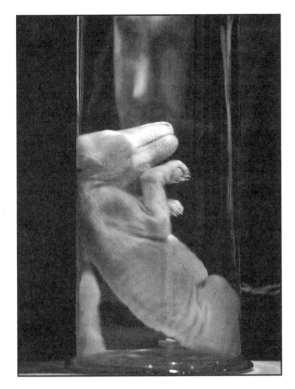

Before You Read

Answer the following questions.

1. What do you know about cloning? What kinds of animals have been cloned?

_____

_____

_____

2. Have you heard any reports about cloning in the news recently? If yes, what?

_____

_____

_____

3. Do you know of any animals that have gone extinct? Why did they become extinct?

_____

_____

_____

Target Vocabulary

Match each word with the best meaning.

1. _____ atom

2. _____ coincidence

3. _____ duplicate

4. _____ extinct

5. _____ legislation

6. _____ mammal

7. _____ prohibit

8. _____ reproduce

9. _____ sample

10. _____ technical

a. a law or laws

b. a single thing that shows what a larger group is like

c. related to a specific area of science or technology

d. the smallest possible amount of a chemical element

e. the happening of two or more similar events at the same time by chance

f. to ban by order or law

g. to make copies of something; to have babies

h. to make an exact copy (v); an exact copy (n)

i. not alive, completely dead (for a species of animal or plant)

j. a warm-blooded animal with females that feed milk to their young

When Scottish scientists created the first cloned **mammal**, a sheep named Dolly, in 1996, they certainly opened an ethical can of worms. Many people believe that cloning represents man's attempt to "play God," and want to see it banned. Since the cloning of Dolly, several countries, including the United States, Britain, and Japan, fearing that humans would be next
5 to be cloned, have passed **legislation prohibiting** the cloning of humans.

There are also many who say that cloning research involving other animals should be banned as well. One scientist who doesn't go along with this point of view is Michael Archer, director of the Australian Museum. Archer supports a proposed project to try to bring back the extinct Tasmanian tiger. He believes people "played God" by killing off all of the Tasmanian
10 tigers, but through cloning the mistake could be corrected.

The Tasmanian tiger, also known as the thylacine, was not actually a tiger. In fact, it was more closely related to Australia's kangaroos and koalas because, like these other marsupials, females had a pouch[1] for raising their young. People called this animal a tiger because of the stripes along the animal's back. But it was also called by other names including the Tasmanian
15 wolf, the zebra wolf, and the opossum hyena.

Before the 1800s, this animal could be found all across Australia. But when settlers from Europe came to Australia, they found that Australia was a very good place to raise[2] sheep. Unfortunately, many of these sheep were killed by Tasmanian tigers, so people began to hunt the tigers. There was even a law passed that said the government would pay people who
20 turned in dead Tasmanian tigers. By the 1930s it looked like all of these animals might be killed, so the law was changed to protect them. But it was too late. In 1936, the last known Tasmanian tiger died in a zoo in Tasmania, the same year the law was passed to protect them. Since that time, no evidence has been found of any living Tasmanian tigers in the wild, although many people over the years claim to have seen one.

25 But a surprising discovery was made in 2001. A jar containing a preserved Tasmanian pup[3] was found in the Australian Museum. The jar had been sitting in the museum since 1866! And by a lucky **coincidence**, the pup had been preserved in alcohol rather than another kind of preservative. The alcohol did not destroy the pup's DNA,[4] so that gave researchers the idea to try to use genetic material from the pup to clone a Tasmanian tiger.

30 Books and movies like *Jurassic Park* have made cloning look easy, but in reality, researchers say they are a long way from actually cloning an **extinct** animal. The only currently living cloned animals came from experiments on living species. In these experiments, the eggs that grew into the cloned animals developed inside host mothers of that same species. But since there are no living female Tasmanian tigers to act as mothers, a different species would need
35 to act as the host mother. Researchers need to learn a lot more about the possibilities of this process before any extinct species can be cloned. The project achieved its first breakthrough in 2002 when they managed to make **duplicates** of **sample** genes from the pup—the first step towards **reproducing** the full DNA of the animal. To help the museum with its goal, the state government of New South Wales has established a fund to raise money for the project.

40 "What Professor Mike Archer and his team are attempting is as scientifically exciting and **technically** challenging as splitting the **atom** or landing a man on the moon," said Maurice Paleau, the producer of a television documentary on the cloning efforts.

 _____ **minutes** _____ **seconds** (628 words)

---

[1] **pouch** a bag-like pocket of skin
[2] **raise** (children, animals, etc.) to grow plants or animals; to help a child to grow up
[3] **pup** a baby dog, seal, Tasmanian tiger, or some other animals
[4] **DNA** deoxyribonucleic acid, which carries genetic information for living things

Reading Comprehension

Circle the letter of the best answer.

1. What is the main purpose of the passage?
   - **a.** arguing against cloning research
   - **b.** contrasting cloning laws in different countries
   - **c.** explaining a specific cloning project
   - **d.** presenting the history of cloning research

2. Why are researchers interested in cloning the Tasmanian tiger?
   - **a.** They want to bring the species back to life.
   - **b.** The tiger is useful for controlling sheep populations.
   - **c.** The tiger's fur is valuable for trade.
   - **d.** There are only a few Tasmanian tigers alive today.

3. What caused most of the Tasmanian tigers die?
   - **a.** a disease
   - **b.** larger animals
   - **c.** humans
   - **d.** They were captured for research.

4. How is it possible to clone the Tasmanian tiger?
   - **a.** by catching one of the few animals left in the wild
   - **b.** by changing the law to protect them
   - **c.** by having a female Tasmanian tiger act as a host mother
   - **d.** by using cells from a dead Tasmanian tiger

5. Which of the following can be assumed from the reading?
   - **a.** Archer is very close to creating the first cloned Tasmanian tiger.
   - **b.** People in New South Wales will create a larger zoo.
   - **c.** The cloning laws in New South Wales are very strict.
   - **d.** The government of New South Wales supports this research.

Idioms

Find each idiom in the story.

1. **(open a) can of worms**—*(say or do something to introduce) a controversial topic*
   - The teacher really **opened a can of worms** when he asked the class their opinions on the death penalty.
   - Please don't say anything about politics during dinner. I try to avoid **opening that can of worms** around my parents.

2. **a long way from**—*be far away from (in time or distance)*
   - The country is **a long way from** solving its economic problems.
   - Even after finishing her research, she was still **a long way from** completing her thesis.

3. **bring back**—*reintroduce something from the past*
   - The film *Jurassic Park* is about a man who **brings** dinosaurs **back** from the dead.
   - The novel **brought back** memories of my childhood in the country.

Vocabulary Reinforcement

A. Circle the letter of the word or phrase that best completes the sentence.

1. A water molecule is made of one oxygen and two hydrogen _____.
   a. atoms   **b.** mammals   **c.** samples   **d.** fluids

2. The government will introduce _____ regarding a new tax law.
   a. coincidence   **b.** legislation   **c.** samples   **d.** species

3. I basically understood his experiment, but I couldn't follow all the _____ details.
   a. duplicate   **b.** extinct   **c.** prohibited   **d.** technical

4. Mice _____ very quickly—their population can increase very rapidly.
   a. duplicate   **b.** reproduce   **c.** prohibit   **d.** split

5. The issue of corporate responsibility is a _____ I'd rather not open at this time.
   a. can of worms   **b.** long way   **c.** lucky coincidence   **d.** point of view

6. Visitors are reminded that taking pictures is _____ in the museum.
   a. duplicated   **b.** preserved   **c.** retained   **d.** prohibited

7. I just found out that we were both born on the same day. What a _____!
   a. can of worms   **b.** rule of thumb   **c.** turn for the worse   **d.** coincidence

8. I hope his comments about Australia did not _____ you.
   a. settle   **b.** bring back   **c.** offend   **d.** infect

B. Complete the passage with the correct form of items from the box. One item is extra.

a long way from	coincidence	bring back	duplicate	extinct	mammal	sample

One research team is trying to (1)_____ a(n) (2)_____ animal called the Tasmanian tiger. This (3)_____ was not really a tiger, but it did have stripes on its back. Although the Tasmanian tiger died out in the 1930s, a(n) (4)_____ of the animal's DNA was recovered from a preserved pup found in 2001. So far the team has managed to (5)_____ genes from the tiger pup, but the project is still (6)_____ creating a living cloned animal.

What Do You Think?

1. Should Archer continue his research? What are some of the arguments for and against the project?

2. If you could bring back one extinct animal, what would you bring back, and why?

Review 11-15

A. Circle the correct answer for each question.

1. Which are you more likely to brush up on? **a.** vocabulary **b.** furniture
2. Which word best describes an earthquake? **a.** devastating **b.** malicious
3. Who is more likely to be interviewed for a job? **a.** a culprit **b.** a candidate
4. Which would most people prefer to retain? **a.** a disease **b.** good health
5. Who is more likely to work in an embassy? **a.** an ambassador **b.** an immigrant
6. Which is sometimes described as "a dish best served cold"? **a.** a can of worms **b.** revenge
7. Which are you more likely to seek? **a.** a penalty **b.** a high-paying job
8. Which of these is it better to boast about? **a.** failure **b.** success
9. Which would most people prefer to turn up? **a.** lost keys **b.** bad luck
10. You are more likely to be convicted if you are . . . **a.** innocent **b.** guilty

B. Complete the paragraph with the correct form of items from the box. Two items are extra.

| bring back | culprit | do away with | extinct | intense | mammal |
| point the finger at | pose a problem | preserve | retain | supposedly | thanks to |

The largest land (1)_____ alive today is the elephant. Today, there are two kinds of elephant—the African elephant and the Indian elephant. However, this has not always been the case. Until about 10,000 years ago, there was another group—the mammoths—who unfortunately are now (2)_____. Mammoths, who lived in the (3)_____ cold of northern Russia and North America, looked very similar to modern elephants, but had long hair over their whole bodies.

Some scientists (4)_____ humans as the (5)_____ responsible for the extinction of the mammoths—(6)_____ because mammoth bones have been found in places where humans lived. However, (7)_____ recent evidence, it now seems that changes in weather were most likely responsible. The climate changed, and with it, the types of plants available, (8)_____ for the mammoths, who now had trouble finding food. These changes probably took place quite suddenly, and in fact, whole mammoths have been found perfectly (9)_____ in the ice.

Because mammoths and modern elephants are so similar, some scientists think it might be possible to (10)_____ the animals by mixing DNA taken from frozen mammoths with that of an elephant.

C. Circle the odd one out in each group.

1. **a.** capture   **b.** convict   **c.** arrest   **d.** release
2. **a.** supposedly   **b.** evident   **c.** obvious   **d.** clear
3. **a.** malicious   **b.** devastating   **c.** fatal   **d.** generous
4. **a.** penalty   **b.** reward   **c.** fine   **d.** punishment
5. **a.** culprit   **b.** victim   **c.** criminal   **d.** convict
6. **a.** ambassador   **b.** museum   **c.** academy   **d.** embassy
7. **a.** reproduce   **b.** duplicate   **c.** copy   **d.** unique
8. **a.** ethnic   **b.** immigrant   **c.** local   **d.** foreign
9. **a.** innocent   **b.** malicious   **c.** law-abiding   **d.** honest
10. **a.** raise eyebrows   **b.** be alert   **c.** pay attention   **d.** keep an eye on

D. Use the clues below to complete the crossword.

Across

3. a country's office in another nation
7. Not being able to speak Russian is going to _____ a problem for you when you go to Moscow.
8. put someone off something; discourage
10. She studied the violin at the _____ of music.
13. a person who moves permanently to another country
14. That newspaper doesn't publish real news, only _____ stories about unimportant things.
17. come out of a hidden place; appear
18. No one ever invites her to events. She often feels _____. (2 words)

Down

1. His style of dancing is very _____ and graceful.
2. It's difficult to stay _____ when you are very tired.
3. The job of the police is to _____ the law.
4. the smallest possible unit of any element, e.g., iron, or calcium
5. look for
6. Many people would like the government to _____ smoking in restaurants.
9. keep; not get rid of
11. a situation when everything is disorganized and rules aren't enforced
12. e.g., cow, dog, rat, whale

13. Many _____ people have been sent to prison for crimes they didn't commit.
15. I'm sorry I was rude. I didn't mean to _____ you.
16. join; combine; put together

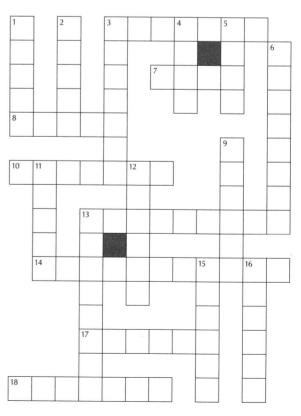

Jim Thompson: Life and Legend

Before You Read

Answer the following questions.

1. Do you know of any famous people who have died or disappeared mysteriously? What do you think happened to these people?

_____

2. Do you know anyone who has started their own business? If yes, what kind of business?

_____

3. What do you know about Thailand? What kinds of products is it famous for?

_____

Target Vocabulary

Match each word with the best meaning.

1. _____ assemble
2. _____ authentic
3. _____ exquisite
4. _____ intelligence
5. _____ intrigued
6. _____ persuade
7. _____ revive
8. _____ rival
9. _____ scheme
10. _____ supplement

a. a competitor
b. a plan (often a secret or dishonest plan)
c. perfect; beautiful; very finely made
d. secret information about a country or enemy
e. to cause someone to believe or do something by arguing or talking with them
f. genuine; real
g. interested and curious
h. put something together; make; construct
i. to reawaken; to give new energy to; to begin to use or do something again; bring back
j. to make an addition or additions to

On Easter Sunday 1967, Jim Thompson was on vacation in Malaysia. While staying in the Cameron Highlands, he stepped out for a walk alone through the jungle. And that was the last anyone ever saw of him. It was as though he had vanished into thin air. To this day, no clues have been found as to what happened to this wealthy American businessman who is credited with
5 single-handedly **reviving** the Thai silk industry.

Thompson was born in the United States in 1906. He studied architecture and worked for several years before joining the army to fight during World War II. He was sent to Thailand, where he worked with a United States **intelligence** agency. It was this first taste of life in the Far East that changed Thompson's life. When the war ended, he decided to leave the army and move to
10 Thailand permanently.

At first, Thompson planned to renovate a famous hotel in Bangkok, the Oriental Hotel, to attract tourists. That project eventually fell through, but by that time Thompson had already hit upon another business **scheme** that would eventually make him a millionaire.

While traveling around Thailand, Thompson came across what he considered **exquisite** samples
15 of handwoven[1] Thai silk. At that time, weaving silk by hand was almost an extinct art in Thailand. Very few people were interested in doing it, and even those weavers still at work only did it on the side as a **supplement** to their regular income from other work. However, Thompson was **intrigued** by the silk he found and began seeking out other weavers and their samples.

Eventually his search led Thompson to Ban Krua, a very poor district in Bangkok alongside one of
20 the canals[2] running through the city. In Ban Krua, Thompson found a whole community of weavers living very close to each other. Although Thailand is by and large a Buddhist country, these weavers were Muslim—a fact that helps explain why they all stayed together within their tight community to support one another. Thompson was so impressed with the material being woven in this village that he took samples to show fashion magazines in New York. These
25 magazine writers were amazed with the quality of this silk and wanted more.

Thompson returned to Ban Krua with orders for more silk. At that time, most of the weavers in Ban Krua supported themselves through other jobs, but Thompson eventually **persuaded** them to go back into production to supply his new company, the Thai Silk Company Ltd, founded in 1948. This company soon made both Thompson and a few of the Ban Krua weavers very wealthy.

30 As his business continued to grow, Thompson began to explore other interests. He began collecting works of art and building his own house. But Thompson did not just build an ordinary house. He wanted a uniquely Thai house. He searched the country for **authentic** Thai houses representing the best examples of old Thailand. Six of the houses he found were then brought together and **reassembled** into a single home, which Thompson finally moved into in 1959. Today
35 the house is both a historical treasure and attraction for Thai people and visitors to Bangkok. Not only is it a beautiful house inside and out, but it is also filled with the works of art Thompson collected during his travels.

As for Thompson's disappearance, although no hard evidence has been found, there are many theories explaining Thompson's fate. Some say he was captured and killed by Chinese
40 communists. Others think he was murdered by gangsters or **rival** business owners. And there is one theory that says he met a local woman and is now living in the jungle with her. Perhaps he simply died in the jungle from falling into a hidden cave or hole, or being eaten by a tiger. If his body was eaten by wild animals, it would explain why no trace of the Thai Silk King has ever been found.

 _____ **minutes** _____ **seconds** (658 words)

---

[1] **handwoven** weaving is making fabric by crossing threads over and under each other. The prefix "hand-" means it is done by hand, rather than in a factory.
[2] **canal** a waterway, often dug by workers for boats to carry goods and passengers

Reading Comprehension

Circle the letter of the best answer.

1. What is the main subject of the reading?
   a. the development of the Thai silk industry
   b. how Thompson improved weaving techniques
   c. one man's life and mysterious death
   d. a unique house and collection of Thai art

2. When did Thompson first go to Thailand?
   a. as a child   **b.** as a college student   **c.** as an adult   **d.** as an old man

3. What did Thompson find in Ban Krua?
   a. a factory that made Thai silk
   b. a large, exquisite house
   c. beautiful clothes made of Thai silk
   d. people to help his business

4. Which statement about Thompson's house is true?
   a. It has a single big room inside it.
   b. It looks ordinary from the outside.
   c. Thompson never actually lived in it.
   d. It was made from several old houses.

5. What is the writer's main point in the final paragraph?
   a. No one is sure what happened to Thompson.
   b. Thompson was murdered.
   c. Thompson was probably eaten by animals.
   d. He is possibly still alive and hiding.

Idioms

Find each idiom in the story.

1. **credit someone (with something)/give someone credit (for something)**—*say someone did or played a major part in some good thing*
   • Many people **credit** the new president **with** saving the economy.
   • The conservation organization was **credited with** saving many endangered species from extinction.

2. **fall through**—*to have plans fail before reaching a final goal*
   • We were hoping to travel to Europe, but our plans **fell through**.
   • The negotiations between the two companies may **fall through** if they can't agree on the price.

3. **on the side**—*as a secondary job or hobby; not as one's main source of income*
   • She works in an office, and writes poetry **on the side**.
   • His main job was managing a supermarket, but he enjoyed repairing cars **on the side**.

Vocabulary Reinforcement

A. Circle the letter of the word or phrase that best completes the sentence.

1. He was _____ by the first page of the story, so he continued reading.
   a. revived   **b.** intrigued   **c.** persuaded   **d.** retained

2. If you don't eat well enough, you might need to _____ your diet with vitamins.
   a. assemble   **b.** supplement   **c.** revive   **d.** prohibit

3. No one could get near the burning building because of the _____ heat.
   a. authentic   **b.** rival   **c.** tight   **d.** intense

4. In wartime, the side with the best _____ has a large advantage.
   a. intelligence   **b.** scheme   **c.** spokesperson   **d.** gossip

5. The article _____ Ms. Wilson with making the school one of the top schools in the country.
   a. credits   **b.** blames   **c.** approves   **d.** persuades

6. The two boys compete on every test. They are _____ for the highest score.
   a. communities   **b.** intelligence   **c.** ambassadors   **d.** rivals

7. These are _____ ancient Roman coins.
   a. authentic   **b.** intrigued   **c.** assembled   **d.** extinct

8. Furniture from this shop is cheaper, but you need to _____ it yourself.
   a. assemble   **b.** revive   **c.** persuade   **d.** deter

B. Complete the passage with the correct form of items from the box. One item is extra.

intelligence	exquisite	fall through	on the side	revive	scheme	supplement

While living in Thailand, Jim Thompson fell in love with the (1)_____ handwoven silks he saw there. After Thompson's original (2)_____ for making money in Thailand (3)_____, he came up with the idea of marketing Thai silk. The problem was finding a group of weavers willing to work full time. For most weavers at the time, weaving was just something they did (4)_____ as a way to (5)_____ their income. But Thompson managed to set up his business, and (6)_____ the Thai silk industry.

What Do You Think?

1. What do you think really happened to Thompson?

2. If you were going to start a business, what kind of business would it be? Where would you locate it?

The Great Illusionist

Before You Read

Answer the following questions.

1. Can you, or can anyone you know, perform any magic tricks? If yes, what?

_____

_____

_____

2. Do you know any famous magicians? What kind of magic tricks are they famous for?

_____

_____

_____

3. What do you know about the man in the photograph? What is he doing?

_____

_____

_____

Target Vocabulary

Match each word with the best meaning.

1. _____ accomplish
2. _____ criticize
3. _____ endorse
4. _____ endurance
5. _____ feat
6. _____ ordeal
7. _____ protest
8. _____ spring up
9. _____ starve
10. _____ stunt

a. to complain because something is wrong or unfair

b. to point out the faults in someone or something

c. to suddenly appear

d. to finish; to achieve

e. to approve an idea, act, or product

f. an impressive act, showing strength, bravery, or unusual ability

g. a painful experience that tests one's abilities

h. to feel pain or die from going without food

i. the ability to do something properly over a long period of time

j. a difficult or dangerous action

David Blaine calls himself an illusionist—a kind of magician who appears to do spectacular and often dangerous tricks. Among his more widely publicized **feats**, Blaine has been buried alive for a week, spent sixty hours encased in a hollow block of ice, and spent thirty-five hours standing on a platform 50 centimeters in diameter at the top of a 30-meter high pillar.

5 In 2003, the thirty-year-old illusionist from New York spent forty-four days in a clear plastic box that was hanging from a crane above the Thames River in London. But there was more to this trick than just staying in a small box for such a long time. Blaine also went without food for the entire period, living on nothing but water the whole time.

On the day Blaine entered the box and the crane lifted him high above the river, a crowd of
10 curious spectators gathered to watch. For the next six weeks the crowds continued to drop by the site to watch Blaine sleeping, writing in his journal, and staring back at them. However, not everyone just wanted to watch. Some people came to give Blaine a hard time and to do things to break the magician's will and force him to come down. A few people threw things at his box or grilled food under it so that the smell would float up to the starving performer.
15 One person even went so far as to try and cut the hose carrying water up to Blaine's box, but security guards stopped the vandal before he could do any damage.

Finally, after forty-four days up in the air, Blaine was lowered to the ground and released from his box. He was weak and much thinner than before, but the performer still managed to give a short speech to the crowd gathered to watch him emerge. Then he was put in an
20 ambulance and rushed to a hospital where he spent the next week recovering from his **ordeal**.

Not everyone in the crowd was satisfied with the ending of the magician's **stunt**. They had come expecting to see a more dramatic finale. Some of the suggestions for ending the feat in a spectacular way included dropping the box into the river and watching Blaine escape, or opening the box in the air and letting Blaine jump out. Or, in a true magician's fashion, some
25 people wanted to see him vanish into thin air, leaving a white rabbit in his place.

So what did David Blaine finally **accomplish** through this amazing feat of **endurance**? He certainly generated a lot of headlines! Along with a number of articles appearing in newspapers on both sides of the Atlantic, various web sites **sprang up** both supporting and **criticizing** the man and his stunt. And an estimated 250,000 people viewed Blaine in person
30 by actually visiting his location beside the Thames. In addition, about 2.5 million people tuned in to watch live broadcasts of Blaine over his forty-four-day ordeal on British television.

However, one thing Blaine has not accomplished over his amazing career is setting a world record. Even from the outset, the Guinness Book of Records said they would not consider Blaine's forty-four days over the Thames for any kind of record. In the first place, a
35 spokesperson for Guinness said the publication does not **endorse** people **starving** themselves as an endurance feat. As the spokesperson explained, "If a person beats the old record and then dies, is the attempt successful?"

And in the second place, people have gone without solid food and have also stayed in smaller spaces for longer than forty-four days. In the 1970s, a prisoner in England went for 385 days
40 without solid food to **protest** against his conviction. Doctors fed him through a tube into his stomach. And in 1997, a man in South Africa stayed in a barrel one-eighth the size of Blaine's box for sixty-seven days. So, although his feat was certainly amazing, Blaine still has a long way to go to make it into the record books.

_____ **minutes** _____ **seconds** (673 words)

Reading Comprehension

Circle the letter of the best answer.

1. What is the passage mainly about?
   - **a.** an amazing television show
   - **b.** an extraordinary feat
   - **c.** how magicians do magic
   - **d.** why Blaine became an illusionist

2. Which of Blaine's stunts lasted the longest?
   - **a.** being buried alive
   - **b.** being trapped in ice
   - **c.** standing on a platform
   - **d.** sitting in a box

3. What did people NOT do while he was in the box?
   - **a.** cook things near him
   - **b.** cut his water hose
   - **c.** stand by the river and watch him
   - **d.** throw things at him

4. Why did some people criticize his trick?
   - **a.** Blaine came out of the box early.
   - **b.** The end was boring.
   - **c.** Blaine tricked them.
   - **d.** The tickets to see him were too expensive.

5. According to the passage, which of the following adjectives does NOT describe Blaine?
   - **a.** record-breaking
   - **b.** controversial
   - **c.** intriguing
   - **d.** publicity-seeking

Idioms

Find each idiom in the story.

1. **from the outset**—*from the beginning; from the start*
   - **From the outset**, he was against the suggestion to change the club's name.
   - The product sold well **from the outset**.

2. **give someone a hard time**—*annoy or bother someone*
   - She always **gives** her brother **a hard time** about his weight.
   - The other players **gave** the new team member **a hard time** during his first day at practice.

3. **go so far as to (do something)**—*do something extreme for a purpose*
   - I would never **go so far as to** call him a liar, but I don't trust everything he says.
   - Some of the fans **went so far as to** buy tickets online for $500 each!

Vocabulary Reinforcement

A. Circle the letter of the word or phrase that best completes the sentence.

1. The company asked a famous athlete to _____ their product.
   a. accomplish   **b.** criticize   **c.** endorse   **d.** protest

2. Hiking across the desert after their plane crashed was a terrible _____ for the family.
   a. endurance   **b.** feat   **c.** stunt   **d.** ordeal

3. The group plans to _____ the government's new law limiting free speech.
   a. protest   **b.** accomplish   **c.** satisfy   **d.** spring up

4. Let's stop working and have lunch. I'm _____.
   a. endorsed   **b.** enduring   **c.** grilled   **d.** starving

5. Some students went _____ to work all night to finish their essays on time.
   a. from the outset   **b.** a hard time   **c.** so far as   **d.** to lengths

6. Before you spend a lot of money on a handwoven rug, you should make sure that it's _____.
   a. authentic   **b.** criticized   **c.** exotic   **d.** evident

7. We didn't plan to meet each other today, but we met downtown by _____.
   a. ordeal   **b.** scheme   **c.** coincidence   **d.** alert

8. In order to lock the building by 6:15, the conference organizers decided _____ to stop at exactly 6 P.M.
   a. by coincidence   **b.** from the outset   **c.** a long way from   **d.** unsuspectingly

B. Complete the passage with the correct form of items from the box. One item is extra.

accomplish   feat   starve   criticize   endurance   give him a hard time   endorse

David Blaine is a man who has done many amazing (1)_____ stunts over his career. For one of his latest (2)_____, he stayed inside a small box and (3)_____ himself for forty-four days. Lots of people visited the site of his ordeal—some to watch Blaine, and others to (4)_____. But Blaine (5)_____ the stunt without suffering any serious harm. However, he did not set a world record, because the Guinness Book of Records had said from the outset that they would not (6)_____ his record attempt.

What Do You Think?

1. Do you think that Blaine accomplished anything by performing this stunt? If yes, what? If no, what do you think was his main purpose for completing the ordeal?

2. What is the most impressive magic trick you've seen? How do you think it was done? Do you think it is possible that some people have magical abilities?

Giants

Before You Read

Answer the following questions.

1. What do you think is the average height of people in your country?

   _____

   _____

   _____

2. Who is the tallest person you know? How tall is he or she? How tall do you think was the tallest person ever?

   _____

   _____

   _____

3. What do you think are the advantages and disadvantages of being very tall?

   _____

   _____

   _____

Target Vocabulary

Match each word with the best meaning.

1. _____ anatomy
2. _____ coffin
3. _____ exaggerate
4. _____ nevertheless/nonetheless
5. _____ nickname
6. _____ plausible
7. _____ province
8. _____ span
9. _____ stimulate
10. _____ tip

a. a division of a country, similar to a state

b. to increase energy or activity

c. the end of something long and narrow

d. in spite of that; however

e. to say that something is better, worse, more important, etc. than it really is

f. the measure of space across something from one point or side to the other (n); to stretch across from one point to another (v)

g. (the study of) the structure of living things, e.g., muscles, bones, nerves, etc.

h. seeming to be true, logical, or reasonable

i. an informal name given to a person in addition to a legal one

j. a box-like container in which a dead person is put for burial

Many cultures around the world have legends about giants—people who are taller and stronger than normal humans. Famous legendary giants include the one who chased Jack down the beanstalk in the children's tale, as well as Goliath, who fought with David in a famous account from the Bible. Goliath was said to be 274 centimeters tall, and supposedly he could spread his
5 arms 290 centimeters wide! Biblical historians say that Goliath was in fact real. However, an early Greek translation of the Bible reveals that Goliath was only 183 centimeters tall, with an arm **span** of around 213 centimeters. These measurements seem much more **plausible** according to what we now know of human growth and **anatomy**.

There have been proven cases in history of people who have grown to unnatural sizes. However,
10 true giants in history are few and far between. Many of the cases must be viewed with some doubt because people (and even doctors) have been known to **exaggerate** every now and again. **Nevertheless**, some people do indeed grow to be giants. The pituitary gland,[1] a small gland in the brain, is responsible for producing growth hormone[2] in children. Sometimes this gland gives off too much of the hormone, and children grow uncontrollably larger than normal.

15 The Chinese basketball player, Yao Ming, one of the tallest players to ever play in the United States NBA,[3] is 229 centimeters tall. However, he doesn't even come close to Robert Wadlow, a true giant. Mr. Wadlow was born on February 22, 1918, in a small town in Illinois. By the time he was thirteen years old, Mr. Wadlow was 218 centimeters tall—much taller than his fellow classmates at school. At seventeen years old, he was just over 244 centimeters! At the time of his death on July
20 15, 1940, Mr. Wadlow, whose **nickname** was "the Gentle Giant" because of his friendly personality, was measured to be 272 centimeters tall with a shoe size of 47 centimeters, and his hands measured 32 centimeters from his wrist to the **tip** of his middle finger. The **coffin** in which Mr. Wadlow was buried had to be specially made. It measured 328 centimeters in length, and needed twelve men to carry it. On the day of Mr. Wadlow's funeral, all the businesses in his
25 hometown closed in respect, and over 40,000 people signed the guest books at his funeral.

The tallest living woman is Sandy Allen, an American born in 1955, who is 232 centimeters tall. Although very tall, Ms. Allen doesn't reach the height of the tallest woman ever. This was Zeng Jinlian of Yujiang village, Hunan **province** in central China, who was born in 1964 and died at the early age of seventeen. All through her life, Ms. Zeng suffered from scoliosis (a condition where a
30 person's backbone is curved) and could not stand up straight. She began her abnormal growth when she was only four months old, and she grew to a height of 152 centimeters before her fourth birthday. By the time of her death, Ms. Zeng reached a total height of 249 centimeters, if she were measured standing straight up. Her hands were 25 centimeters long, and her feet were 36 centimeters long. In comparison, her parents and her brother were all of average size.

35 Unfortunately, people who grow to these unnaturally large sizes face various physical problems from their condition. The hormone that **stimulates** the natural growth of these people makes their bones grow at a faster rate during childhood, but the hormone does not give any added muscle growth. Therefore, true giants are not very strong. Also, their bodies aren't as resistant to disease as other people. Although it is possible for children who suffer from conditions of abnormal growth to
40 receive medical treatment, these treatments have not had very high success rates in the past.

Sandy Allen, who is over forty-five years old, realizes that her days may be numbered. "My time could be running out," she says. "But I'll go down fighting." She has a nightshirt that says it all: "Life's short, I'm not."

_____ **minutes** _____ **seconds** (680 words)

---

[1] **gland** small organ that produces and sends out chemicals in the body
[2] **hormone** chemical from body organs that stimulates activity in living systems
[3] **NBA** National Basketball Association

Reading Comprehension

Circle the letter of the best answer.

1. According to the passage, which statement about Goliath is true?
   a. He was 274 centimeters tall.
   b. He was 183 centimeters tall.
   c. He fought many people.
   d. He never really existed.

2. According to the passage, why do some people grow to be giants?
   a. Their doctors exaggerate their true height.
   b. They have a problem with their resistance to disease.
   c. They have taken too many hormones.
   d. There is a problem with one of their glands.

3. How old was Robert Wadlow when he died?
   a. 17   b. 22   c. 32   d. 47

4. Which of these physical problems is NOT a side effect of being a giant?
   a. increased physical strength
   b. lowered resistance to disease
   c. a shorter lifetime
   d. All of these are side effects.

5. According to the passage, which of these statements about giants is true?
   a. They are usually more intelligent than other people.
   b. They are usually very gentle people.
   c. They can have surgery to become average height.
   d. They are less likely to live to an old age.

Idioms

Find each idiom in the story.

1. **few and far between**—*rare; unusual*
   - Products of this quality are **few and far between** today.
   - Since she moved overseas, Sally's opportunities to visit her parents were **few and far between**.

2. **(every) now and again**—*occasionally; now and then*
   - I love traveling with my family, but **every now and again** I like going away by myself for a few days.
   - Most movies these days are only average, but **every now and again** a truly great one comes out.

3. **(someone's or something's) days are numbered**— *something will not survive or be successful for much longer*
   - From the day humans first arrived in Mauritius, the dodo's **days were numbered**.
   - After Laura's big argument with the boss, her **days** at the company **were numbered**.

Vocabulary Reinforcement

A. Circle the letter of the word or phrase that best completes the sentence.

1. Careful! You just hit me with the _____ of your umbrella.
   a. tip **b.** span **c.** stunt **d.** fluid

2. Painting my house was a really demanding job. _____ I quite enjoyed it.
   a. Every now and then **b.** Nevertheless **c.** From the outset **d.** As long as

3. Becky was _____ when she said she was very close friends with the President.
   a. dominating **b.** stimulating **c.** assembling **d.** exaggerating

4. His full name is Richard, but everyone calls him by his _____, Dick.
   a. tip **b.** span **c.** nickname **d.** coffin

5. The _____ of that bridge is almost five hundred meters.
   a. province **b.** span **c.** atom **d.** anatomy

6. I'm not sure whether to believe her or not, but her story sounds _____.
   a. plausible **b.** few and far between **c.** exquisite **d.** evident

7. People are cutting down trees so quickly in that forest that its _____.
   a. exaggerated **b.** days are numbered **c.** every now and again **d.** fallen through

8. Mushrooms always _____ under that tree after it rains.
   a. span **b.** accomplish **c.** spring up **d.** enforce

B. Complete the passage with the correct form of items from the box. One item is extra.

anatomy	coffin	exaggerate	few and far between
every now and again		province	stimulate

From what doctors know about human growth and (1)_____, it seems that (2)_____ children grow to unnatural sizes. Doctors even know the gland in the body that (3)_____ this growth. There are quite a few people alive today over two meters tall, but true giants taller than this are (4)_____. The tallest man in history was 2.72 meters tall, and he had to be buried in a special (5)_____ when he died. The tallest woman, who was from a(n) (6)_____ in central China, only lived for seventeen years. But she was 2.49 meters tall when she passed away.

What Do You Think?

1. Do you think it would be more difficult to be very tall or very short? Why?

2. Does your country have any legends about people who are abnormally tall or strong? What happens in the legend?

Women's Basketball

Before You Read

Answer the following questions.

1. What sports are popular with women in your country?

_____

_____

2. Do you know any famous female athletes? Are there any famous female athletes from your country?

_____

_____

3. Have you ever seen a women's basketball game?

_____

_____

Target Vocabulary

Match each word with the best meaning.

1. _____ adapt/adaptation

2. _____ demanding

3. _____ distinction

4. _____ dominate

5. _____ federation

6. _____ indoor

7. _____ qualify

8. _____ revise

9. _____ superior

10. _____ zone

a. a clear difference

b. a group of organizations or states

c. an area marked for a special purpose

d. a person who is higher in importance (n); better (than), above average (adj)

e. challenging; requiring great effort

f. located inside a building

g. to change and correct something

h. to have the most important place or greatest influence; to control

i. to pass tests to show one's ability for something

j. to change; to function in a new way; to adjust (v); a change (n)

Women's basketball has been played for almost as long as men's basketball. In 1891, Canadian-born Dr. James Naismith organized the first basketball game at the International YMCA College at Springfield, Massachusetts. As the story goes, Dr. Naismith's **superiors** at the college asked him to come up with an **indoor** game for the young men to play during the winter months when it
5   was too cold to go outside. It was hoped that organizing such a game would give the youths a chance to let off steam in positive ways, rather than causing trouble at the school during the long months of winter.

The next year, after reading an article describing Naismith's game, Senda Berenson, a physical education instructor at Smith College, decided to **adapt** the game for her female students.
10   Berenson's adaptation divided the court into three playing areas, and the girls were required to stay within their assigned areas. This was done to make the game less physically **demanding** and "more suitable for women." As other colleges began to create their own women's basketball teams, rules were constantly being **revised** and rewritten. But even while coaches[1] and officials continued to play around with the rules, the popularity of the sport spread.

15   Basketball's popularity not only spread across North America, but also around the world. By the 1950s, both men's and women's basketball national championships were being played in countries across Europe, Asia, and South America. The **Federation** International de Basketball Amateur (FIBA) held its first women's basketball world championship in Chile in 1953, three years after the first men's world championship was held. Since then, FIBA has held this
20   championship tournament between the best women's basketball teams around the world once every four years. The FIBA matches occur in even-numbered years between the years when the Olympic Games occur. And in 1989, FIBA did away with the **distinction** between amateur and professional athletes. This decision allowed professional female basketball players to join national teams for the FIBA championship.

25   Just as soccer teams must **qualify** for the World Cup, women's basketball teams compete with other international teams to qualify for the FIBA championship. Only sixteen teams get the chance to play in the competition. FIBA organizes qualifying matches within five **zones** worldwide: Africa, Asia, Europe, the Americas, and Oceania. At least one team from each zone qualifies to represent that zone for the championship competition.

30   Over the years, the teams from two countries have **dominated** the FIBA women's championships. Of the fourteen championships between 1953 and 2002, the team from the United States won seven times and the team from the Soviet Union won six times. Only in 1994 did the championship title go to a team from a country other than the United States or the Soviet Union. That year, Brazil defeated the People's Republic of China in the final match 96-84.

35   In 2003, FIBA began a new women's basketball competition in addition to its regular championship for women. The competition held in 2003 was the World Championship for Young Women, in which no athletes over the age of twenty-one competed on any of the national teams. This competition, also called the Women's Basketball World Cup, is held every year rather than once every four years. The team from Samara, Russia, where the tournament was held, won
40   the first World Cup competition by defeating a team from the United States by 72-68.

_____ **minutes** _____ **seconds** (563 words)

---

[1] **coach** a trainer or teacher, e.g. for individuals who are studying sports

Reading Comprehension

Circle the letter of the best answer.

1. What is the main idea of this reading?
   a. Women's basketball is more challenging than men's basketball.
   b. Women basketball players aren't as good as male basketball players.
   c. America is the strongest country for women's basketball.
   d. Women's basketball is a serious sport with a long history.

2. Why were the rules for women's basketball originally different from those of men's basketball?
   a. to make the game shorter
   b. to make the game more challenging
   c. to make the game easier
   d. to make the game more interesting

3. Which statement about the FIBA women's basketball world championship is true?
   a. It is only for women under twenty-one.
   b. It is held every year.
   c. It is only for amateur athletes.
   d. It always involves at least one team from Africa.

4. According to the passage, FIBA will hold a women's basketball championship in . . .
   a. 2008   b. 2009   c. 2010   d. 2011

5. According to the passage, which country has never won the FIBA women's basketball championship?
   a. the United States
   b. the Soviet Union/Russia
   c. China
   d. Brazil

Idioms

Find each idiom in the story.

1. **play around with**—*to try different ways of doing something to find the best solution; test something*
   - You should **play around with** a few different cameras to see which one you like before you buy.
   - I **played around with** lots of different ideas before I decided on a topic for my thesis.

2. **just as**—*in exactly the same way as*
   - **Just as** most families today have a car, in the future, people will probably have flying machines.
   - **Just as** humans use their hands to pick things up, elephants use their trunks.

3. **let off steam**—*get rid of anger or energy through physical activity*
   - After the rain stopped for the first time in a week, the children ran outside to **let off steam**.
   - I'm sorry I yelled at you. I was just stressed and **letting off steam**.

Vocabulary Reinforcement

A. Circle the letter of the word or phrase that best completes the sentence.

1. What is the _____ between a giant and someone who is just very tall?
   a. zone   **b.** revision   **c.** qualification   **d.** distinction

2. After years of study, she finally _____ as a doctor.
   a. qualified   **b.** exaggerated   **c.** revised   **d.** dominated

3. Look! Your keys are on the table, _____ I told you.
   a. now and again   **b.** just as   **c.** evident   **d.** from the outset

4. The book was heavily _____ for the second edition.
   a. superior   **b.** qualified   **c.** revised   **d.** starved

5. Lily's _____ at work always give her a hard time.
   a. superiors   **b.** dominators   **c.** critics   **d.** mammals

6. The no-fly _____ is an area above the country in which planes are not allowed to fly.
   a. province   **b.** zone   **c.** span   **d.** distinction

7. I can't get my computer to work. Could you please _____ it and see if you can fix it?
   a. play around with   **b.** let off steam with   **c.** revise   **d.** qualify

8. I'm really interested in your idea. It sounds _____.
   a. demanding   **b.** exaggerated   **c.** authentic   **d.** intriguing

B. Complete the passage with the correct form of items from the box. One item is extra.

adapt	demanding	dominate	federation	just as	let off steam	indoor

The man who invented the game of basketball, Dr. James Naismith, was looking for a way for boys to (1)_____ during the long winter months. Because it was cold outside, the boys had to play some kind of (2)_____ sport, so Dr. Naismith came up with basketball. The next year, a female professor (3)_____ the rules to make the game less physically (4)_____ for women. Shortly after that, basketball spread around the world. By the 1950s, the international men's and women's basketball (5)_____ were holding world championship matches. Over the past fifty years, the American and Russian teams have (6)_____ the women's championships, but that may change in the future.

What Do You Think?

1. Do you think that women's sport is taken less seriously than men's sport in your country?

2. Why do you think that the American and Russian teams have been so strong in women's basketball? What can a country do to become stronger in international sport?

From Elvis to Eminem

Before You Read

Answer the following questions.

1. What kind of music is popular in your country?

   _____

   _____

   _____

2. How is today's music different from popular music in the past?

   _____

   _____

   _____

3. Who do you think is the best-selling band of all time? What about the best-selling solo artist?

   _____

   _____

   _____

Target Vocabulary

Match each word with the best meaning.

1. _____ authority
2. _____ compilation
3. _____ debut
4. _____ enthrall
5. _____ generation
6. _____ harsh
7. _____ idol
8. _____ plenty (of)
9. _____ solo
10. _____ weird

a. a celebrity, such as a film or music star

b. a good supply of; more than enough

c. any of the different age levels in a family; a group of people of approximately the same age

d. by oneself; alone

e. an expert or master in a particular subject; power, control

f. severe

g. something produced by bringing together many different things

h. strange; bizarre (usually negative)

i. to appear for the first time (v); a first appearance (n)

j. to hold someone's attention completely

Reading Passage

Every **generation** has its own unique taste in music and fashion. Although some trends make a comeback from time to time, there is no denying that the sounds of modern music are very different from the music of the past. And typically, the sounds of "today" are **harshly** criticized by music lovers of the songs of yesteryear.

5 There were **plenty of** critics of rhythm and blues (R & B) music in the 1930s and 1940s. And when R & B evolved into rock and roll, the criticism as well as the music just got louder. The older generation could not understand why kids were so **enthralled** by all the noise of the drums and electric guitars or by the singers with **weird** hairstyles and strange clothes. Then in 1954, Elvis Presley made his **debut** and changed the history of modern music. With his good

10 looks and fresh sound, he captured the imagination and hearts of young people around the world. But Elvis did not change history because of his musical genius; rather, he changed history by showing the music industry how a pop **idol** could make millions.

Although no completely accurate figures are available, Elvis is surely the most successful **solo** artist in history. Over his career, he had more than 170 major hit singles and more than 80

15 successful albums. Seventy of these albums went platinum, selling more than one million copies each. According to Billboard, a U.S. magazine regarded as the **authority** on the music industry, Elvis remains the most successful solo performer with nine number one albums. In 2003, twenty-six years after he passed away, Elvis earned over $40 million—making him the top earning dead celebrity of that year.

20 If one singer could make such a mark on music history, then a group of singers could leave an even stronger mark. And such a group came along in the early 1960s—the Beatles. This band of four young men from Liverpool, England, went on to become the most successful musical group in history. Estimates of Beatles recording sales are assumed to be well over one billion copies worldwide. And after the group broke up, each member of the band went on to sell

25 millions more records over their solo careers.

Additionally, the popularity of the Beatles did not die out just because the band members went their separate ways. In 2000, a new Beatles album was released with twenty-seven old hits from the group. The album was called "1" and it was a smash hit. The first week it was released, it went to number one on the Billboard chart, and it stayed there for nine weeks.

30 Including this album, the Beatles set a new record for the most number one albums by any singer or group, with nineteen—more than twice the number of number one albums Elvis had.

But the evolution of rock and roll and modern music did not end with the Beatles. Other singers and bands have emerged over the years and left their own marks on the music industry. For example, an American band from the 1970s called the Eagles still holds the

35 record for the best-selling album of all time in the United States. Their greatest hits **compilation** album has sold more than twenty-seven million copies to date domestically.[1] In terms of global sales, however, the Eagles' album is exceeded by Michael Jackson's *Thriller* from the 1980s, which has sold more than forty-seven million copies worldwide.

From Elvis to the Beatles to Michael Jackson, clearly musical tastes have changed a lot over

40 the years. In fact, by the late 1990s the hottest music was neither rock nor pop, but rather rap and hip-hop. With over nineteen million copies sold of his first three albums, American rapper Eminem appears to be well on his way to becoming the next superstar of modern music.

_____ **minutes** _____ **seconds** (642 words)

---

[1] **domestically** relating to national concerns, i.e. excluding foreign

Reading Comprehension

Circle the letter of the best answer.

1. What is the best title for this passage?
   - **a.** Superstars of Popular Music
   - **b.** Top-Selling Singles of All Time
   - **c.** Elvis Presley—the Man, the Legend
   - **d.** The History of Rhythm and Blues

2. According to the passage, what was NOT an early criticism of rock and roll?
   - **a.** It was noisy.
   - **b.** The singers had bizarre hairstyles.
   - **c.** The bands dressed strangely.
   - **d.** The performers earned too much money.

3. According to the passage, what was Elvis's biggest impact?
   - **a.** He showed that a performer could become extremely rich.
   - **b.** He influenced Eminem.
   - **c.** He introduced the electric guitar.
   - **d.** He introduced young people to R & B.

4. What is NOT true about Elvis's career?
   - **a.** He is the best-selling solo singer to date.
   - **b.** He sold more than 70 million albums.
   - **c.** In the last year of his life he earned $40 million.
   - **d.** More than 150 of his singles were successful.

5. Which singer or group has had the largest number of best-selling albums?
   - **a.** The Beatles   **b.** The Eagles   **c.** Michael Jackson   **d.** Elvis Presley

Idioms

Find each idiom in the story.

1. **make/leave a/one's mark**—*become noticed or famous for doing something impressive*
   - He's only been at the company for a year, but he's really **made a mark** with all the hard work he's done.
   - The professor really **left his mark** on the students he used to teach.

2. **to date**—*until now*
   - My parents have been on vacation for three weeks, and **to date** I haven't even gotten a postcard from them.
   - The band's latest CD has been its biggest-selling one **to date**.

3. **go (their) separate ways**—*separate; go to different places; end a relationship*
   - After the conference finished, everyone **went their separate ways**.
   - The couple finally decided to split up and **go their separate ways**.

Vocabulary Reinforcement

A. Circle the letter of the word or phrase that best completes the sentence.

1. My aunt is a(n) _____ on Chinese art.
  a. idol   **b.** authority   **c.** compilation   **d.** rival

2. This book is a _____ of stories by many different writers.
  a. compilation   **b.** distinction   **c.** generation   **d.** plenty

3. The teenage girls waited outside the theater to see their _____.
  a. solo   **b.** authority   **c.** debut   **d.** idol

4. This travel guide is aimed specifically at the _____ traveler.
  a. harsh   **b.** weird   **c.** solo   **d.** extinct

5. I was so _____ by the television program that I didn't hear the phone ring.
  a. enthralled   **b.** compiled   **c.** endorsed   **d.** duplicated

6. Mary is a(n) _____ name for a male dog.
  a. enthralling   **b.** weird   **c.** demanding   **d.** exquisite

7. There's too much work for me to finish alone. I'll see if I can _____ my superiors to help me.
  a. persuade   **b.** enthrall   **c.** adapt   **d.** convict

8. The lifeguards rescued the drowning man and managed to _____ him.
  a. leave a mark on   **b.** dominate   **c.** revive   **d.** intrigue

B. Complete the passage with the correct form of items from the box. One item is extra.

debut	generation	harsh	idol	leave his mark	plenty of	to date

Styles of fashion and music change with each new (1)_____. And often, the new styles meet with (2)_____ criticism from older people. For example, parents complained about Elvis, but he found (3)_____ fans to buy his records. Elvis went on to (4)_____ on the history of music by becoming the greatest solo artist of all time. Then the Beatles made their (5)_____ in the 1960s and eventually became the greatest musical group of all time. Decades after going their separate ways, the Beatles compilation album "1", released in 2000, became a top-selling album, giving the group a total of nineteen number one albums (6)_____.

What Do You Think?

1. Which singers or bands performing today do you think will still be popular ten years from now? Are there any bands or singers today that you think will still be important fifty years from now?

2. Do you think that style and appearance are more important than talent for performers today? Who do you think is talented, and who do you think is popular mainly for style or appearance?

Review 16-20

A. Circle the correct answer for each question.

1. Which is a province more likely to have? **a.** a capital **b.** a federation
2. A controversial decision is more likely to be . . . **a.** protested **b.** endorsed
3. Which is an example of an anatomical feature? **a.** a river **b.** a nose
4. Which would most people rather be? **a.** superior **b.** dominated
5. Which of these might be found in a compilation? **a.** songs **b.** countries
6. A diamond necklace is more likely to be described as . . . **a.** weird **b.** exquisite
7. Which of these needs to be assembled? **a.** a model plane **b.** a recipe
8. Which kind of guest do hotel employees prefer? **a.** demanding **b.** intriguing
9. Which kind of criticism is worse? **a.** mild **b.** harsh
10. Before handing in an essay, it may need to be . . . **a.** qualified **b.** revised

B. Complete the paragraph with the correct form of items from the box. Two items are extra.

accomplish	debut	demanding	endurance	enthrall	feat
generations	nickname	idol	persuade	plausible	play around with

The large crowds of people who came to see David Blaine's performance in London in 2003 show that magicians are incredibly popular. However, although David Blaine is famous, his popularity is still a long way from that of Harry Houdini, who has been the (1)_____ of many magicians for (2)_____.

Harry Houdini was the (3)_____ of Ehrich Weiss, who was born in Hungary in 1874 and moved to the United States as a child. He made his (4)_____ performance as a professional magician in 1891, but at first he wasn't very popular. His early tricks were just card tricks and other traditional acts, but he soon started (5)_____ escape (6)_____. These escape stunts led to his big breakthrough, and he soon took his show to Europe where plenty of people were (7)_____ with his show. One of his most (8)_____ stunts was called "The Chinese Water Torture," where he was chained and hung upside-down in a locked glass and steel container of water. He (9)_____ his escape while the audience watched his ordeal inside the tank.

After the death of his mother, Houdini spent the last few years of his life revealing as frauds people who claimed to be able to speak to the dead. These frauds, with their (10)_____ lies, tricked many mourning people, and he wanted to persuade the public that they were just magicians like him. Houdini died in 1926 as the result of an illness.

C. Circle the odd one out in each group.

1. **a.** ally   **b.** rival   **c.** competitor   **d.** enemy

2. **a.** authentic   **b.** genuine   **c.** real   **d.** fraud

3. **a.** coffin   **b.** tomb   **c.** idol   **d.** grave

4. **a.** scheme   **b.** ordeal   **c.** feat   **d.** stunt

5. **a.** federation **b.** solo   **c.** alone   **d.** single

6. **a.** debut   **b.** initial   **c.** first   **d.** repeat

7. **a.** plausible   **b.** believable   **c.** realistic   **d.** sensational

8. **a.** zone   **b.** area   **c.** era   **d.** region

9. **a.** adapt   **b.** remain   **c.** evolve   **d.** change

10. **a.** weird   **b.** bizarre   **c.** typical   **d.** abnormal

D. Use the clues below to complete the crossword.

Across

4. Fans of the high school football team were very pleased when their team beat the _____ school.

5. She was the first woman to sail _____ around the world—with no help from anyone.

6. The young pianist was very nervous before his _____ performance.

8. Please take a pen if you need one. I have _____ extra ones. (2 words)

11. I really love that singer—she's my _____.

12. The winter this year was very _____ and all the plants in my garden died.

14. White fur is a very useful _____ for animals that live in the snow.

16. This is a great product—it is _____ to the competitors in every way.

17. Swimming across the English Channel is a difficult _____.

Down

1. If your plans for this weekend _____, give me a call and we'll go out. (2 words)

2. The teacher was _____ by her students for giving too much homework.

3. The parachutists landed in a special _____ on the grass.

5. Jumping over the edge of the waterfall was a dangerous _____.

7. The survivors had a terrible _____ after their ship sank.

8. I'll try to _____ my husband to come to the party on Saturday.

9. interest; excite; hold someone's attention intensely

10. In some countries you can be arrested if you _____ against the government.

11. Completing jigsaw puzzles is a very popular _____ hobby.

13. Tomato ketchup and ice cream is a(n) _____ combination to eat together.

15. He poked me with the _____ of his cane.

World Map

Countries ● *and places* ○ *mentioned in the readings:*

Europe
1. Belgium
2. Denmark
3. England
4. *Liverpool*
5. *London*
6. *Thames River*
7. Finland
8. France
9. *Paris*
10. Germany
11. Greece
12. Italy
13. *Rome*
14. Netherland
15. Northern Ireland
16. Norway
17. Russia
18. *Samara*
19. Scotland
20. Spain
21. Sweden
22. *Varmdo*
23. Switzerland
24. Wales

Africa
25. Egypt
26. Mauritius
27. South Africa

Asia/Australasia
28. Australia
29. *New South Wales*
30. *Tasmania*
31. China
32. *Hong Kong*
33. *Hunan*
34. India
35. Indonesia
36. *Borobudur*
37. *Java*
38. Japan
39. *Kobe*
40. *Tokyo*
41. Korea, Republic of
42. *Seoul*
43. Malaysia
44. *Cameron Highlands*
45. Mongolia
46. Philippines
47. *Manila*
48. Thailand
49. *Bangkok*
50. Vietnam

North America
51. Canada
52. Mexico
53. *Mexico City*
54. *Oaxaca*
55. United States of America
56. *Hollywood*
57. *Illinois*
58. *New York*
59. *Springfield, Massachusetts*
60. *Van Nuys, California*

South America
61. Argentina
62. *Buenos Aires*
63. Brazil
64. Chile

Vocabulary Index

Words and phrases included in the Target Vocabulary and Idioms sections are listed below. The number refers to the Unit in which the word or phrase first appears. Idioms are shown in *italics*.

Author's Acknowledgments

I would like to acknowledge Ki Chul Kang for his inspiration and guidance. I would also like to acknowledge Ji Eun Jung for her honest feedback from the student perspective. Finally, I have to acknowledge all of those students who inspired me to seek out materials to suit the interest of a variety of readers. It was both enjoyable and instructive for me as a teacher and a writer.

I am also grateful to the following teaching professionals who gave very useful feedback as the second edition was being developed.

Casey Malarcher

Andrew White	Induk Institute of Technology, Seoul, South Korea
Chris Campbell	Congress Institute, Osaka, Japan
Claudia Sasía	Instituto México, Puebla, México
Corina Correa	ALUMNI, São Paulo, Brasil
Evelyn Shiang	Tung Nan Institute of Technology, Taipei, Taiwan
Gail Wu	Overseas Chinese Institute of Technology, Taichung, Taiwan
Iain B.M. Lambert	Tokyo Denki University, Tokyo, Japan
Jaeman Choi	Wonkwang University, Chollabukdo, South Korea
Karen Ku	Overseas Chinese Institute of Technology, Taichung, Taiwan
Lex Kim	Lex Kim English School, Seoul, South Korea
Lucila Sotomayor	Instituto D'Amicis, Puebla, México
Marlene Tavares de Almeida	WordShop, Belo Horizonte, Brasil
Pai Sung-Yeon	Charlie's International School, Seoul, South Korea
Pauline Kao	Tung Nan Institute of Technology, Taipei, Taiwan
Richmond Stroupe	World Language Center, Soka University, Tokyo, Japan
Robert McLeod	Kang's Language School, Seoul, South Korea
Sherri Lynn Leibert	Congress Institute, Tokyo, Japan
Shwu Hui Tsai	Chung Kuo Institute of Technology, Taipei, Taiwan
Taming Hsiung	Chung Kuo Institute of Technology, Taipei, Taiwan